John C. R. Colomb

The Defence of Great and Greater Britain

sketches of its naval, military, and political aspects

John C. R. Colomb

The Defence of Great and Greater Britain
sketches of its naval, military, and political aspects

ISBN/EAN: 9783337073039

Printed in Europe, USA, Canada, Australia, Japan

Cover: Foto ©ninafisch / pixelio.de

More available books at **www.hansebooks.com**

THE DEFENCE

OF

GREAT AND GREATER BRITAIN.

SKETCHES OF ITS NAVAL, MILITARY, AND POLITICAL
ASPECTS;

ANNOTATED WITH EXTRACTS
FROM THE DISCUSSIONS THEY HAVE CALLED FORTH
IN THE PRESS OF GREATER BRITAIN.

BY
CAPTAIN J. C. R. COLOMB, F.S.S., F.R.G.S.,
AND FELLOW ROYAL COLONIAL INSTITUTE.

With a Map.

LONDON:
EDWARD STANFORD, 55, CHARING CROSS, S.W.
—
1880.

PREFACE.

As a Royal Commission, limited in its nature and local in its constitution, is now sitting to investigate portions of the subject of the following pages, I am induced to lay them before the general reader.

In doing so I venture to offer the facts they contain to the earnest attention of those whose broad national sympathies and instincts are superior to the provincial prejudices of political partizanship.

J. C. R. C.

DROUMQUINNA, KENMARE,
December 1879.

CONTENTS.

		PAGE
MAP	to face title	
TEXT OF ROYAL COMMISSION		viii

CHAPTER I.
INTRODUCTORY AND POLITICAL 1

CHAPTER II.
THE NAVY AND THE COLONIES 14

CHAPTER III.
COLONIAL DEFENCE 35

CHAPTER IV.
IMPERIAL AND COLONIAL RESPONSIBILITIES IN WAR 93

CHAPTER V.
NAVAL AND MILITARY RAW RESOURCES OF THE COLONIES .. 157

CHAPTER VI.
NAVAL AND MILITARY DEVELOPED RESOURCES 200

APPENDICES.

No. I.—EXTRACT FROM THE NAVAL PRIZE ESSAY, BY CAPTAIN P. H. COLOMB, R.N. 249

„ II.—EXTRACT FROM LECTURE BY GENERAL COLLINSON, R.E. 257

„ III.—EXTRACT FROM LECTURE BY LIEUT.-COL. STRANGE, R.A. 259

Extract from 'Gazette,' 12th September, 1879.

DOWNING STREET, *September 9th,* 1879.

THE Queen has been pleased to issue a Commission under Her Majesty's Royal Sign Manual to the effect following:—

* * * * *

Whereas we have thought it expedient, for divers good causes and considerations, that a Commission should forthwith issue to inquire into the condition and sufficiency of the means both naval and military, provided for the defence of the more important sea-ports within our Colonial Possessions and their dependencies, and of the stations established or required within our said possessions and dependencies for coaling, refitting, or repairing the ships of our Navy, and for the protection of the commerce of our Colonies with the United Kingdom of Great Britain and Ireland, with each other, and with foreign countries:

And whereas it is expedient to consider and determine in which of our stations and ports it is desirable, on account of their strategical or commercial importance, to provide an organized system of defence, in addition to such general protection as can be afforded by our Naval forces; and whether such defence should consist of permanent works manned by garrisons of Imperial or local troops, or both combined, or of any local naval organization or other armaments and appliances:

And whereas it is desirable to consider whether, and in what proportions, the cost of such measures of defence should be divided between the Imperial Government and the Colonies to which they relate, or should be wholly defrayed by the Imperial Government or by the Colonies:

Now know ye that we, reposing great trust and confidence in your zeal, knowledge, and ability, have authorized and appointed, and do by these presents authorize and appoint you, the said Henry Howard Molyneaux, Earl of Carnarvon, Hugh Culling Eardley Childers, Sir Henry Thurstan Holland, Sir Alexander Milne, Sir John Lintorn Arabin Simmons, Sir Henry Barkly, Thomas Brassey, and Robert George Crookshank Hamilton to be our Commissioners for the purpose of such inquiries as aforesaid, and that you may offer such suggestions as may seem to you meet as to the best means (regard being had to the works completed and in progress, and to the ordinary number of our naval and military forces voted by Parliament) of providing for the defence and protection of our Colonial Possessions and commerce as aforesaid, special attention being given to the necessity of providing safe coaling, refitting, and repairing stations in such of our Colonial Possessions and their dependencies as you may deem best suited for the requirements of our fleet and mercantile marine in time of war.

DEFENCE
OF
GREAT AND GREATER BRITAIN.

CHAPTER I.

INTRODUCTORY.

For the first time in the history of our Empire we are about to inquire—How to defend it? The fact of our taking such a great and unprecedented step has attracted but little notice; " a suspected murder at Richmond " would command infinitely more. Proof is thus furnished of the necessity for such inquiry, for the comparative silence with which the official announcement was received by the home press and public indicates how little the multitude knows of what concerns it most. It is therefore desirable it should be encouraged to learn, and though a Royal Commission may be little more than a convenient political " limbo " for inconvenient questions, it is nevertheless a great public instructor; it collects authentic facts, and by their subsequent publication knowledge is increased and attention awakened.

It is possible the larger portion of " the public "

do not even know that there is an intimate and indissoluble connection between the state of the defences of particular colonial ports (respecting which the Commission is to inquire) and the personal safety of the inhabitants of Great Britain and Ireland. Did the people of the United Kingdom believe this public inquiry concerned their own individual interests so closely, the announcement of the Commission would, doubtless, have at once received a warmer welcome. It is, therefore, unhappily necessary to explain that, according to the terms of the Commission, its fundamental object may be thus shortly expressed :—

1. To inquire and report on the steps necessary to adopt to ensure that in war the people of these islands shall not be starved into submission, and that the communications of Great with Greater Britain shall not be cut.

2. To consider how the burden of cost resulting from taking these necessary steps should be apportioned between Great and Greater Britain?

There are thus two apparently distinct problems submitted to the examination of the Commission; each concern Great and Greater Britain, though widely different in their nature.

Having shortly explained the nature of inquiry, in order to draw attention to its extreme importance, it is further necessary to offer preliminary remarks on each of the two questions submitted to its consideration.

As regards the first,—This is a strategical problem, the complexity of which only arises from the fact of its necessarily involving both naval and military considerations, and its scope is only limited by the waters of the world.

That our Empire should have drifted often perilously near whirlpools of war, without any inquiry into so obviously necessary provisions for its safety, is perhaps the most remarkable feature of its naval and military history. The only justification perhaps for such criminal neglect, is the memory of a naval past so brilliant and so dazzling as to render it difficult to see clearly those things on which *now* depends our naval future; seeing nothing, we have refused to believe that there could be as regards " naval supremacy," any question at all. Our national naval policy thus became simply a policy of blind trust. While the Royal Commission on National Defences in 1859 calmly left " the extended commerce," and consequently the food supply of Great Britain, to the protection of the fleet ; a select Committee of the House of Commons, 1861, declared Greater Britain must, for its defence, " trust mainly to naval supremacy." Without pausing to inquire into the altered conditions and principles requiring fulfilment to enable naval power to perform the twofold task then and in the future, the Empire took a new departure, and with these two reports as its passports set out on a voyage of purely military discovery. The adventures of a naval Empire in search of a purely military career, are at once painful and instructive; and it is interesting to note that the "intelligent Zulu" has shaken more than one belief; for public confidence in Lord Cardwell's schemes for securing British safety by purely military means—regardless of either naval requirements or colonial arrangements—received a severe check at St. Vincent, and finally collapsed in the bush of South Africa. Meantime, while the public has been dreaming of a military future and of proud honour yet to be won by driblets of half-trained English boys conquering great hosts on imaginary battle-fields somewhere in Asia Minor or Eastern Europe, British commerce has been extending and Greater Britain developing, and the official *Gazette* calls us back to reflect that after all we are not a military nation but a great naval Empire, and are quite in the dark as to its necessities, even under the known circumstances of modern naval warfare, and have been wilfully blind to those commonplace requirements which are essential to British safety.

It is for these reasons it appears desirable to submit to the consideration of the general public the following chapters. They deal with the subject, now about to be officially and publicly investigated, and are selections from many similar efforts during past years,* purposely framed with the express object of obtaining this public inquiry, and

* Commencing 1866.

in this respect they have the merit of an entirely practical, yet partial, success. Practical, because the inquiry for which they strove has been granted, and the nature of this inquiry officially committed to the Commission is identical with that herein defined as necessary,* and, as will be seen, persistently advocated throughout these writings; partial, because the composition of the Commission is essentially and most disappointingly different. Greater Britain is left out in the cold, without any representation on the Commission which is to determine questions vital to her various interests.

Returning, however, to the primary question to be investigated by this Commission, and with which the text of the following chapters deals, the reader is warned that the views so put forth rest upon the assumption that we are an Empire, and that it is essential, not only to "British interests," but to the civilization and peace of the world, we should remain so. It may, in the eyes of some, be almost a crime to use the word Empire to describe the British position; it may even be a matter of opinion whether, in a political sense, the aggregate of colonial interests over which Queen Victoria reigns can be properly described by the word Empire, but it is a matter of fact that, taking the mother country and her colonies together, no other word than Empire describes our geographical position; nor can it be denied that the people of this geogra-

* Vide pp. 32, 87, 97, &c.

phical Empire have as much right to assert a united claim to a common nationality as the people of Bulgaria, for example, and therefore should be prepared to preserve it. If this be admitted, it follows, as a matter of course, that British duty necessitates the taking of ordinary precautions for the defence of our geographical Empire *as a whole*, and then are we led to the direct conclusion that British defence must be Imperial both in its objects and its nature. Doubtless the question is hugely wide; but it is hoped the following chapters will sufficiently show that by the practical application of simple first principles, the broader features of its solution are in no way beyond the comprehension of the most ordinary mind. The real value of these papers entirely depends upon whether the first principles are true? and whether they are truthfully applied? and here the reader must form his own deliberately calm opinion, irrespective of all considerations as to where he may find himself landed by logical conclusions from which—if the premises are correct—there can be no escape. It is necessary, in all humility, to say this; because, unless I misread altogether the popular view and ordinary conception of national defence, we have been in the past, and are even now, apparently led more by fancies than by facts. In 1859, we *fancied* that France furnished a model for British defensive necessities; in 1866, we *fancied* it had become a question whether Prussia did not furnish a better. Sedan firmly established the *fancy* that Germany was the best; but 1879 brings before us the *fact* that Germany has no Greater Germany, and that we are not prepared to protect our commerce, nor even to guard the food supply of these two little islands in war.

When I recall the supremely placid contempt with which some years ago my reasons for urging this inquiry were treated by the popular mind wrapt in such fancies, and the official brain vainly endeavouring to please it, the announcement of a Royal Commission now to hold this very inquiry is but another proof that a little truth may have a great triumph.

Relative to the purely naval, military, and strategical aspects of Imperial Defence, it is not necessary here to say more. Ample materials for serious thought and careful consideration will be found in the text, written as it was in the anxious hope of leading people to think out the question independently for themselves. In passing, however, to a few introductory remarks on the political aspects involved in the problem, which turn mainly on the element of "cost," I must add one remark.

The indulgence of "fancies" in social life is universally acknowledged to be expensive, equally so is it a costly item in national expenditure. A nation, or an Empire, must pay heavily for such indulgence, even though in the end there naturally be very little indeed to show for it.

Not till our war forces are re-organized in a manner perfectly adapted to the necessities of our Empire — exceptionally situated and essentially different from all others in the world—can that great auditor History, "write off" what has been wasted on popular military delusions. Even now, who can accurately estimate what our French, Prussian, and German "*fancies*" have cost us, though all are aware we have uncommonly little, if anything at all, to show for them?

Turning, then, to the next problem submitted to the Commission,—viz. the distribution of the cost of measures necessary, for Imperial safety, between Great and Greater Britain.

It may be fairly described as a constitutional "Gordian-knot," which has taken busy British brains, working in all four quarters of the world, more than a century to tie. They have done their work so well that now only the sword of representation can ever cut it. Those of my readers who do not accept this assertion are referred to the notes to the following pages, which give in her own words the views of Greater Britain on the all-important matter of cost and its control. These notes are simply extracts from the discussions which Chapters III. and IV. raised in the press of Greater Britain.* These expressions of

* None are appended to Chapters V. and VI., as the Institution, before which they were delivered as lectures, excludes politics from its discussions; to attach, therefore, political criticisms to these chapters would neither be respectful nor proper.—J. C. R. C.

opinion are the utterances of the only voice Greater Britain at present has in Imperial policy; on this ground alone these notes should command earnest and respectful attention. It is only by and through the press of Greater Britain, we at home can know what are the hopes and fears of her people in respect of Imperial policy, in the direction of which she is constitutionally dumb, though equally concerned. She sits now voiceless at the feet of that Gamaliel whose abode is at Westminster, whose latest exploit is the discovery that childish obstruction is an Imperial power, and whose chief characteristic is apparently a compound of hysterical excitement in the presence of national danger, with a morbid craving for microscopic introspection when it has passed away. This lawgiver, on whose wisdom the fate of Greater Britain hangs, may speak words of peace to her comfort, or of war to her peril, she has only in silence and humility to obey. What is it to her that an Indian budget or Colonial bill ever finds the halls deserted where Imperial wisdom dwells? let it be enough for her to know that a question on the "state of Rotten Row" crowds them from floor to roof.

But even this Gamaliel cannot stop the progress of the world, and while Greater Britain sits silently pondering outside the doors of the huge vestry of Westminster, the balance of such power as material resources and commercial prosperity give is quietly but swiftly passing from us to her.

Applying this fact to naval and military considerations, it will be seen in Chapters V. and VI. that we have as yet done practically nothing whatever to prepare for this great change. Though the primary sources of Great Britain's naval and military power are even now, in some respects, overshadowed by the aggregate of those found in Greater Britain, our internal Imperial policy has ignored so important a fact. If it be asked why, the answer is, because the whole problem of defence resolves itself in practice into one cost; cost in its turn resolves itself into taxes; and, as taxes cannot be separated from representation, we are at once brought face to face with the naked fact, that Imperial representation lies at the root of the problem of Imperial defence.

If, then, Greater Britain's resources are to be at the disposal of the Empire, she cannot be debarred from taking her place in its councils. The real question at issue, therefore, is this—Is Great Britain, with increasing pauperism and, relatively, decreasing trade, prepared to face the future *with* its accumulating Imperial responsibilities, but *without* relatively accumulating power at command to meet them?

If she is not, then she must either wriggle out of her responsibilities as best she may, or go honestly into a real partnership with Greater Britain, and abandon the theory that she alone has the brains and the money necessary to carry on an Imperial business both in peace and war. Delay in coming to terms will not diminish the responsibilities of Great Britain, but will increase the resources and the power of Greater Britain, and therefore procrastination only tends to make it more to the advantage of Great Britain, and less to the benefit of Greater Britain, to form such partnership. In any case, Greater Britain will have many words to say on the subject, indeed has much to say now, even on that one aspect of the question—defence. It was, therefore, of extreme importance to let Greater Britain, by means of these notes, speak in the words of its own press direct to the reader of the text. Their distinct utterances will sufficiently warn him that Imperial Defence cannot be settled on any lasting basis simply by naval and military science, and they forbid the vain hope that the Royal Commission—in the composition of which the principle of Colonial representation is excluded—can do more than suggest to Greater Britain what she has a clear right not to accept, and what Great Britain would, were the positions reversed, certainly reject, viz. to pay bills for war purposes without any control over the items, nor any voice in the question which rules the total—peace or war?

A French paper * reviewing Chapter IV., thus tersely expressed the present position of the problem of British Imperial Defence : " Ces impossibilités actuelles sont des impossibilités de législation ; " but it added, " en cas d'urgence il est probable qu'elles seraient promptement résolues." As we, however, cannot look forward with complacency to internal revolution being added to external war, nor for a case of emergency such as would over-ride constitutional government, we should calmly survey our real position now, and hope the force of public opinion may resolve the difficulties of our own creation, which stand in the way of the solution of the problem of Imperial Defence.

It is to be hoped that the Royal Commission now sitting is but a preliminary investigation, a preparation for such measures as shall draw together Great and Greater Britain by a closer and more enduring tie.

The *Gazette* announcement of 12th September, 1879, may perhaps mark a point of new departure in our naval, military, and political history. It is, at all events, an official intimation that the time has come for a great question to descend from the spaceless region of speculative thought, and present itself to the business-like examination of "any three or more commissioners" — just like any ordinary Gas or Sewer Bill! It may vanish back

* *La Liberté Coloniale*, June 17, 1877.

whence it came; or, it may take its place in the arena of practical politics to be torn to pieces in the conflict of local parties, or, perhaps, prove stronger than both by producing new political combinations.

CHAPTER II.

THE NAVY AND THE COLONIES.*

There is but too much reason to fear that neither the Navy nor the Colonies command at present sufficient popular attention. Nine Englishmen out of ten are but too apt to accept the assertions that the Navy is the "right arm of England," and that the colonies are the "glory of the mother country," without any strict examination into the reasons supporting them. Lord Palmerston's declaration that "steam has bridged the channel," is as often repeated as the fact that it has done something infinitely greater is forgotten: it has bridged the water distances which separate the colonies from the mother country and from each other. Those who perpetually dwell upon purely military arrangements necessary to resist invasion take the bridging of the channel by steam for their text; and its truth is undeniable. In 1859, public opinion awoke to the unpalatable conviction that—in the words of the Royal Commission—"The nation cannot be considered as secured against invasion if depending for its defence on the fleet alone." This " Royal Commission on the National

* This chapter originally appeared in the *British Trade Journal*, 1 Jan., 1872.

Defence of the United Kingdom," in 1859, broke down some of our most cherished and time-honoured popular beliefs and prejudices. Those amongst us, however, who remember the course of events and the circumstances which ultimately led to the assembly of that Commission, have doubtless not forgotten that, for years previously, evidence had been accumulating, and men's minds had been working towards the conclusions which that Commission authoritatively expressed. There are signs now on the surface of public thought indicating a tendency to extend the outlook on our preparations for defence beyond the shores of that small portion of our Empire which absorbed all our attention twenty years ago. It may be useful, therefore, to glance at some facts which may assist us in arriving at practical conclusions.

To appreciate their value it is necessary briefly to call to mind the salient features of our defensive arrangements and policy from 1859 to 1879. The first thing of striking importance is the growth of a purely military spirit amongst us, plainly exhibited (1) by the spontaneous action of the nation in arming and organising itself into a volunteer force of some 170,000, binding itself to serve for the defence of Great Britain only; (2) the resuscitation and total re-organization by successive Governments of the Militia and Yeomanry, a force of some 150,000, legally bound to serve only in *Great Britain and Ireland*; (3) the complete re-organization of our regular army—"horse, foot, and artillery"; (4) the construction of splendid fortifications and military works in the United Kingdom, at Plymouth, Portsmouth, Chatham, &c., which did not exist twenty years ago. Now, the whole of these great, extraordinary, and rapid movements in a purely *military* direction spring originally from a feeling of national insecurity, created by the fall of the national confidence in the power of "the wooden walls of old England" to protect these islands from invasion, and the substitution of no amount of thickness of armour for wood can win back that blind and implicit bygone trust so rudely shaken by a practical appreciation of the change produced by steam. But, besides all these solid proofs of the quick growth of a purely military spirit, there are others more subtle, but nevertheless as sure. Most Englishmen would now be ashamed to acknowledge ignorance of the broad features of the military history of recent wars, or the leading principles of military operations. The press and the current literature teem with articles of a purely military nature, and the whole question of national defence is in the vast majority of instances, treated from a purely military standpoint. On the other hand, the Navy, as a sort of abstract quantity of national necessity, absorbs no such popular attention, though the service is, as it deserves to be, most popular. It would be very hard to find an Englishman, unconnected with the service, who is ashamed to say he knows nothing at all of recent naval history, and still less of the broad principles of naval operations and arrangements. The nation gets angry and excited when an ironclad goes to the bottom, and, from ignorance of naval matters, generally blames the wrong man; but, in the intervals between mishaps which must occasionally happen, the popular mind is somewhat lethargic, if not wholly apathetic, in its regard of much that appertains to "England's right arm." It insists it shall be always most powerful, and must, at a moment's notice, be ready to "sweep the sea"; but what really constitutes naval power, or how fleets are to "sweep" the sea in days of steam, it does not care to inquire. There is, further, a remarkable difference in the general method of approaching naval, as compared with military, questions, even in the House of Commons. As a general rule, military questions are dealt with on broad principles. The amount and nature of force required to defend Great Britain, or India, or anywhere else; the proportion of artillery to infantry &c it is possible to discuss with a full House, because the subject is well understood; but all naval discussions generally empty the House, and turn usually on the stability of a particular ship, the thickness of a particular plate, the efficiency of a certain torpedo, or the cost of some shipbuilding material. Naval debates show but too often and too clearly that we are more or less really "at sea" as regards general naval principles. We are but too apt to excuse ourselves by attributing all our naval difficulties to the "advance of science," but we have never applied ourselves to ascertain whether these difficulties are real or imaginary, or whether they are not aggravated, if not originated, in the decline of national interest in naval affairs, resulting in a neglect to seek out and define general principles of naval policy. To sum up the results of our national defensive efforts of the past twenty years, it may be said, as regards the army, we have sought out, defined, and carried out the general principles to govern our military arrangements, we have taken every advantage of "advancing science" to improve and perfect the details; but with respect to the Navy we have only used "advancing science" for the improvement of some details, such as ships, without even the faintest national effort to seek out the great general principles which must guide our naval arrangements. This is doubly remarkable when it is remembered that it was the change produced on naval operations by steam that has led us so far afoot towards a purely *military* goal, and caused us, so to speak, to turn our back on those new naval principles which are the very essence of the problem submitted by steam for England's solution.

It would be impossible in the space at command even to *glance* at more than one of these great principles which must guide our naval arrangements in these days of steam, but which, nevertheless, we neglect. Take, for example, the primary element on which all steam fleets must rely—coal. Button-hole the first intelligent-looking gentleman casually met, and ask him to explain what the national arrangements are for the supply of coal to British fleets all over the world in war. No satisfactory reply will be given. Ask any number of Knights of the Shire, and you are tolerably certain to get no explanation. Ask naval officers, and from them you certainly will get information which will hardly be satisfactory. Not many months ago, for example, the Admiral who commanded our China fleet in 1877, Admiral Ryder, stated as follows:—" I have just returned from the command on the Japan and China Station, and with an imminent prospect of war, I felt very doubtful whether I should ever get a pound of coal without taking it forcibly from a neutral." In 1854 a magnificent British fleet steamed away to the Baltic. Her Majesty bade it adieu, and with it went the great heart of England. The Admiral's signal of "Sharpen your cutlasses" is remembered by many, but the fact that the fleet went to one rendezvous while its coal went to another is forgotten by all. Before we blame "advancing science" for the absence of well-defined national naval principles, we should at least take a business-like view of our naval arrangements. The nation is not free from well-deserved reproach if it neglects now to inquire what these arrangements are. In the navy estimates for 1878–79, at page 201, will be seen, among other items, 73,500*l.* charged to Deptford Yard for coals for the fleet abroad; that is all the information given on the subject. Who can picture what momentous issues may hang in war on what is *unwritten* on page 201 of our naval estimates, but on which even now some light is thrown by the above-quoted statement of the Admiral, whose station was bounded on the north by Russian waters, and whose naval base, Hong Kong, is but eight days' steam from the Russian naval base, Vladivostok? It is apparently Japan, or perhaps China, to which the Admiral probably refers under the term "neutral." Taking "coal forcibly" from Japan means conflict with a power possessing a respectable ironclad squadron, or, in the case of China, possessing dockyards, one of which, 117 acres in extent, has all modern appliances, and in ten years has turned out fifteen war steamers, with an aggregate tonnage of 15,000 tons; whose navy is further supplemented with such formidable wasps as the 'Alpha,' &c., built in England. As the annual value of our trade with China and Japan approaches 15,000,000*l.*, the arrangements for supplying and securing to our fleet in war ample supplies of coal is surely a question of very considerable national importance; yet it does not command popular sympathy. But the question of coal supply does not simply concern the power of the British war fleets to keep the sea; on it rests the whole complex operations of our steam trade. Steam companies take care to provide ample fuel for their wants, and store it at the most convenient points along the great highroads of the sea. Though, as a general rule, these vessels have far superior coal-carrying capacity to any of our warships, they are nevertheless dependent on fixed coaling-stations, the great majority of which are on British territory. The main object of hostile cruisers would be to damage our sea trade, and no more effective mode could suggest itself than burning the coals of our steam mercantile fleets. If the defence of these British coal-stores abroad is to be left to sea-going ships, instead of such ships being at their proper places on the high seas, they will be in war snugly lying off the coal wharves. Here is another principle which "advancing science," at all events, does not obscure, but it is not on the programme of present popular favour. There is yet one more principle of naval arrangements to which, while excluding from consideration several others, it may be as well to refer. Were the Horse Guards to send a cavalry force on any expedition without spare horseshoes, or the means of making them, there would be a general outcry; yet the nation silently acquiesces in the dispatch of whole fleets, composed of ships which are complicated masses of intricate machinery, to distant parts of the world without providing them with means of repair, floating or fixed, and does not even provide dock accommodation for war-ships at so important a place as the Cape, commanding as it does the great pass leading from one hemisphere to the other. Having thus indicated roughly some matters really worthy of national consideration, and in no way above the ordinary conception of the least intelligent among us, let us return to another aspect of the results of the past twenty years. Careful examination will show that while our preparations to resist invasion with purely military forces have enormously increased, the possibility of invasion has not in any like proportion increased if measured by the steam transport at command of possible invading powers. If such examination be diverted into another channel, the following curious circumstance is brought to light:—As before remarked, beyond improving the details, such as ships, of our naval arrangements, we have done but little in the direction of naval progress, though during that period the number of our steamers employed in the foreign trade has quietly and noiselessly quadrupled. This means that for every steamer requiring protection in war in 1859 there are now four, and that our trading operations are therefore now four times as dependent on coal as in 1859. In 1859 the total tonnage of British vessels which entered and

cleared at ports in the United Kingdom was
13,000,000 odd; in 1877 it was 53,000,000
odd. We have therefore now four times as
great a national stake on the water as we
had in 1859, at which period we commenced
giving our exclusive attention to purely military
arrangements. It is instructive to think of facts
such as these, and it cannot be too often repeated
that one-half the people of these islands are now
dependent on over-sea transport for food. It is
also a matter for serious reflection that other
nations are making rapid strides in naval development, while two new naval powers, Germany and
Italy, have risen out of the troubled Europe of the
two last decades. We have been so engrossed
with secrets of late military successes, that we are
seemingly in some danger of becoming blind to
what has followed in naval directions. We are
hardly justified in complacently reckoning up the
number of our ironclads and comparing the total
with those of other nations. There is a wide
difference between a purely naval attack on a
nation absolutely dependent on the sea, and a
purely naval attack on a power not so situated.
The defence of innumerable and enormously long
sea-roads, which girdle the globe, is a totally
different problem from that of a simple and single
coast-line. The "advance of science" has, by
producing torpedoes, made that difference all the
greater. Experience has proved them to be of

great efficacy in securing a coast-line from naval attack, but of small account in the defence of a line of communication on the high sea. An extended position, connected by long lines, requires a much greater force to maintain it than to attack it. An insignificant attacking force can harass and worry it, unless the most careful, painstaking attention be paid to strategical laws, based on accurate knowledge, and all arrangements are made subject to those laws. This is as true of sea as of land positions, and it is as applicable to the great sea-roads of our Empire as to the frontiers and passes of Afghanistan. In the one case, however, the general public is an excited and interested student; in the other, merely a careless, indolent spectator of what it does not even profess to comprehend. The extent of our sea commerce is so great that we take Admiralty assertion as to the provision for its adequate protection in war as much on trust as most people do the statements of astronomers respecting the distance of planets from the earth. To most minds it is too fatiguing to attempt to inquire closely into a subject which in area covers all the oceans and seas of the world, and has to deal with millions of tons of shipping carrying cargoes of hundreds of millions of pounds sterling value. Hence it is that our war fleets are scattered, meandering over the globe, and no one apparently knows how in war they are to have supplies of coal, or means of supply and repair, nor on what great principles the whole naval machinery of England is to accomplish the work it will then have to do.

It is the fashion to blame the Admiralty when anything goes wrong; but the nation has yet to define for Admiralty guidance what are the cardinal principles on which naval preparations for war are to be based. It has never insisted upon a public inquiry into the changes in our maritime position produced by steam and by the development of our commerce. It is apparently content to go on in days of steam as it did in days of sail power, and hence it is that we have enormously costly war-vessels carrying but little coal, and huge mercantile steam fleets, while no national movement whatever has been made for the supply of coal to our war fleets when hostilities occur, nor have we taken precautions for the security of the coal depôts of our mercantile fleets when war breaks out. (We have water-roads 13,000 miles in length, commanded by points of British territory, but there is not a place of refuge where helpless merchant ships in war can find even temporary safety or security along their whole length.) The present Admiralty, in preparing to supplement the war navy with the best of mercantile steamers, deserves the gratitude of the nation, which should in return strengthen the hands of that department by insisting that the coals and supplies for the maintenance of our fleets should be adequately and locally protected, so as to leave the fleets free to do their work in guarding the great passes of the ocean. Whether it be the business of the War Office to see to this or not, is a departmental question of infinitely small importance. If England makes up its mind to have the work done, it will not tolerate a paper war between two departments respecting whose business it is to do it. It is evident that as the absolute necessity of arming our mercantile marine in war becomes more apparent, so will the value and importance of our fixed points commanding the great water-roads become more clear as a great element of maritime strength. They must not merely be protected coal depôts, but naval storehouses, where guns, gun-mountings, and ammunition suitable for the use of the mercantile marine can be safely stored. It would be a fatal mistake to attempt to interfere in any shape or form in peace with the internal arrangements of merchant ships for war purposes, if in any way detrimental to their peaceful avocations; and this Mr. Barnaby, the chief constructor, has most happily recognized. It would be, also, simply preposterous to attempt to place in peace any restrictions whatever on the freedom of action, or on the operations of the mercantile marine, in order to provide for the contingency of war. There is hardly any great branch of national industry so exceptionally sensitive of State interference as the shipping trade; none so dangerous a subject for experimental legislation. If, therefore, we are to be prepared—as we undoubtedly must be prepared—to arm our mercantile marine on the outbreak of war, we must recognize the fact that we shall not know beforehand exactly in what part of the world the particular vessels we have selected for the purpose will, at that moment, be found. If we have, say, one hundred of these vessels on the Admiralty list, probably not more than sixty may be at home at any one time. Consequently, if provision for arming them is only to be found in England, two things must happen :—1. Only about one-half of such reserve of ships can be at once armed. 2. The remainder will have either to run the gauntlet home unarmed, or idly wait wherever they may happen to be for armament dispatched from home; and as warlike stores cannot be risked at such a time, armed vessels will have to take them out. Such vessels will, during the performance of that service, be so much deducted from the force available for other duties on the sea. It is very evident, therefore, that [if we are to combine efficiency with economy, and freedom of action of the mercantile marine in peace with its readiness of preparation for war, we must be prepared to arm our mercantile steamers at many points away from home; and the great coaling-stations of our merchant fleet along the lines and at both ends of our sea communications are the most convenient points at which those vessels can be so equipped. Such considerations as these point first to the great colonies, the natural termini of most of our chief water-communications, and next to the smaller intermediate British territories forming stations along the routes.

Before offering necessarily brief remarks on the colonial portion of our subject, it may be instructive to summarize some remarkable changes which, from a defensive point of view, the twenty years just closed has brought about in our colonial history. We have since 1859 withdrawn regular troops from all our great colonies having responsible governments, except the Cape. In the interval which has elapsed the United Kingdom has gone so far as to sell old military clothing and muskets to Canada, while Canada has developed a military system capable of placing 600,000 men under arms, and, as all are aware, has tendered offers of substantial military assistance to us within the last few months. The colonies of Australasia have organized local military forces, and erected defensive works, and the Cape is at this moment engaged in providing military means of internal local defence. The West Indian colonies do not appear to have followed in the same path. The example set by the mother country has not been without its influence on her children, and, therefore, it is not surprising to find that in naval directions little has been done. Canada has provided herself with a naval force of small armed steamers for lake service. Victoria is distinguished by the possession of the 'Cerberus' and 'Nelson,' and a naval establishment of some 350 of all ranks. We may look in vain elsewhere for any advance as regards naval preparations in any of our great colonies at all proportionate either to their military progress or even to their great mercantile development. If we cast our eyes towards India we find the abolition of the Indian navy as the most striking event of our recent Imperial naval history. Passing from this cursory review of colonial and military changes, let us now throw a side-glance at the development of the trade of the four great groups of our Colonial Empire during nearly the same period. In 1859 the total value of exports and imports of Australasia was 48,000,000*l*. odd; in 1876 it was 88,000,000*l*. odd, or nearly double. In 1859 that of British North America was 20,000,000*l*. odd; in 1876 it was over 39,000,000*l*., also nearly double. In 1859 that of our West Indian Islands was 8,000,000*l*. odd, while in 1876 it was nearly 11,000,000*l*. In 1859 that of the Cape was nearly 5,000,000*l*., while in 1876 it was over 11,000,000*l*. It is needless to multiply proofs of the enormously increasing dependence of all parts of the British Empire on the freedom of the sea roads except for the purpose of impressing all Englishmen, home and colonial, with the ever-increasing responsibilities of naval protection. We appear to be in some danger of forgetting that the purely military defence of our Empire *as a whole* must ever be secondary to its naval security. No amount of military force can *swim*, and therefore in an Empire such as ours it can only move to defence or attack through the agency of our mercantile marine under the shelter of sea war-power and sufficient naval strategical arrangements. Putting aside this very interesting question, however, and treating our navy simply as a force for the protection of British sea commerce, the following concluding remarks may serve a useful purpose.

The British navy is furnished, paid, and maintained exclusively by the United Kingdom, but a very large proportion of British sea commerce it will have to protect in war belongs to other parts of our Empire. For example, the number of vessels registered at ports of the United Kingdom is 25,090, with an aggregate of 6,336,360 tons, while the number of vessels registered at ports of the British possessions is 13,158, with an aggregate of 1,797,477 tons. The rest of the Empire, therefore, has on the register of its ports half the total number of ships and about one quarter of the aggregate tonnage of the total British mercantile marine. The gross revenue of British possessions is about equal to that of the United Kingdom; and while the revenue of the United Kingdom is annually charged with some 10,000,000*l*. for the naval protection of British mercantile marine, British possessions are not chargeable with any sum whatever for such protection. India, however, contributes about 69,000*l.* a year on account of the expenses of the fleet on the Indian Station; but the rest of the Empire bears no share of the naval expenses incurred or to be incurred for the protection of its sea commerce in war.

The extraordinary commercial development, progressing by "leaps and bounds," must sooner or later force upon all Englishmen's attention the question of mutual responsibility and mutual effort in the really imperial matter of sea defence. Every year's delay in coming to a common understanding on the subject may possibly render solution more difficult, and there is but too much reason to fear that neglect now may lead the United Kingdom ultimately either to attempt high-handed measures which would surely end in disastrous failure, or towards a blind repudiation of responsibilities which would be the beginning of a lamentable end. It is earnestly to be hoped when this question receives the popular attention it merits that no ill-considered effort will be made to settle it off-hand by any simple " pound, shillings, and pence " arrangement. There are other grave questions behind which forbid such simple mode of dealing with so complex a problem. The strength of the English race does not rest on money-bags; it lies deep in the hearts of a great and free people, who, above all things, love fair play. If, therefore, the extraordinary anomaly respecting naval burdens of Empire is ever to be a thing of the past, it can only satisfactorily result from friendly consultation and reasonable compromise. We must not ask our colonies simply for cash, but we must enlist their active sympathy and practical help in a common effort for a common good. If the foundation-stones of any real system of truly British naval defence are ever to be laid, the colonies must be called into consultation on the matter. We on our part must show real desire to join with them in carrying out, not only systematic and well-defined preparations for ensuring in war the safety of those great water-roads common to us all, but we must do more. We must show our determination to secure them in peace their due proportion of the honour and *prestige* attaching to a great and noble service, as well as those more solid advantages arising from the expenditure of capital and labour incidental to its maintenance. Englishmen are great at compromise, and it is hard to suppose that a truly representative Royal Commission or inquiry into a matter of such vital importance to each and all parts of the Empire would fail to lay down principles ensuring ultimate co-operation and practical success. It is a hopeful sign when men like Mr. Froude, Sir Julius Vogel, Mr. Brassey, M.P., Mr. Donald Currie, General Collinson, Sir E. W. Watkin, M.P., and others are found giving, from various points of view, notes of warning, and it is earnestly to be hoped their voices will not be raised in vain.

When the force of public opinion, home and colonial, grapples the question in a business-like practical manner, the germs of possible combination for naval defensive purposes between England anp. her colonies will probably be discovered in those small neglected points of British territory which command the water-roads of both. Most of them private enterprise has converted into important coaling-stations, and their efficient local protection will, in war, be a matter of common concern to every portion of the Empire. That being so, provision for their safety is a matter in which every part of the Empire is vitally interested. It is more than possible that an expenditure of some 4,000,000*l*. would provide all of them with ample permanent means of necessary local protection. In the case of the great home fortifications, constructed since 1859, the money required was raised by loan. Is the whole British Empire *in combination*, with its gross annual revenue of some 158,000,000*l*., too poor to raise a loan sufficient to protect the points which, in a strategical sense, command its water-roads, and, from a naval point of view, are vital to the power of locomotion both of its war navy and its huge mercantile marine? Let it be remembered that we cannot in war "go down to the sea in ships, nor occupy our business in great waters," save under the fostering care and shelter of armed ships, now absolutely dependent on coal for efficient protective power.

In 1859 we realized the fact that "steam has bridged the Channel." Is 1879 to pass without any visible proof, however slight, of a national recognition of the truth that steam has bridged the water distances which separate the colonies from the mother country?

Finally, it is to be observed that when attempts at invasion are, *in a naval sense*, possible, attempts to cut our sea communications are more than possible; they are even probable, because in the existing state of our naval arrangements and undefined naval principles, the operation involves the application of a much smaller naval-attacking force. We have by the creation of purely military forces, and by the erection of great home fortifications, given in the past twenty years the most ample practical proofs of our national belief in one danger, while during the same period our neglect of naval principles is a striking national memorial of our utter disbelief in the other, perhaps the more real of the two.

CHAPTER III.

ON COLONIAL DEFENCE.*

THOUGH this subject has direct reference to the colonies, it is necessary to observe that "Colonial Defence" cannot be considered as an abstract question, any more than that "National Defence" can be limited in its meaning to the defence of the United Kingdom. The full force of this assertion is not, however, generally understood.

When we get frightened on the subject of what is falsely termed "Our National Safety," but one idea is prevalent in the minds of nine people out of ten, to the exclusion of all other considerations; it is this:—guarding the soil of the British Islands against invasion.

In time of profound peace we like to talk of "our vast Colonial Empire, our extended commerce, and interests in every part of the globe." It sounds big and grand, and, perhaps, some vainly imagine that big swelling words must frighten away aggression; but when danger, real or supposed, threatens, and the nation is alarmed, we habitually forget that "England with her colonies is still a giant amongst nations, and that

* Read before the Royal Colonial Institute, June 28th, 1873.

without them she would be a dwarf," * and exhibit practically our disbelief in the "giant" by seeking refuge in the "arms of the dwarf." †

Look back a few years, and by past events test the truth of this assertion. Take the panic of 1859 and its results. We were in a state of wild alarm. We imagined that France threatened our safety, nay, our existence. We took fright at her successful armies, and her powerful fleets, capable of transporting those armies. We stedfastly shut our eyes to the fact that the possibility of the invasion of England ‡ involves, as a natural con-

---

* *Vide* Sir E. Sullivan on 'Our Economic Catos.'

† **Australia.**—"It is easy enough to defend a dwarf, but then he is only a dwarf. When the English horn of plenty overflows with the rich produce of her far-off climes, and peace has rest for the sole of her foot, then the magnitude and value of her possessions is eloquently acknowledged. Shall it, then, be a reproach to her that in the hour of her adversity she forgot all this, and selfishly looked merely to the protection of her own chalk cliffs and hedgerows? We opine not. We have no reason to believe or even to surmise this. What individual politicians may urge matters little when the will of the people is so easily asserted. The giant will remain a giant in war as in peace."—*Sydney Morning Herald*, June 8th, 1874.

‡ **West Indies.**—"England has grown up to be the greatest maritime power in the world, through her commerce and colonies, quite as much as by the prowess of her arms."—*The West Indian*, April 2nd, 1874.

Canada.—"Twice within a century she has alone and single-handed faced successfully the whole civilized world in arms, and by her naval strategy brought each contest to a glorious as well as profitable conclusion, despite the dense imbecility and gross ignorance of her statesmen and diplomatists; and now when at her nod armies and fleets would arise in every quarter of the globe, manned and commanded by her own sons or their descendants, her politicians and strategists are striving with might and main to confine her force to the defences of the bathing-machines at Brighton, or the buoys and light-ships on the Mersey. The forefathers of the Manchester school of politicians were

sequence, the possibility of investment, the cutting of the Imperial lines of communication, and attacks upon "our vast Colonial Empire, our extended commerce, and interests in every quarter of the globe"; we, in short, forgot everything except our personal safety, and instead of taking measures for defending the Empire, we were satisfied with taking measures for defending the hedgerows of England.

Again, we owe change in our military system to the last panic. We are told by the Government of the day that England (the dwarf) is now better prepared to resist an attempted invasion than during any past period of her history. How has this result been attained? By rendering her colonies and possessions (which swell the dwarf into the giant) less capable of resisting attack.

---

wiser in their day and generation—thoroughly understanding the value of the principle of carrying the war into Africa."—*Volunteer Review*, Ottawa, February 2nd, 1875.

South Africa.—"Sooner or later the subject of Imperial defence will compel attention. At present very few persons, and these men of little real weight in councils of the Empire, bestow any thought upon it. True, we hear much about national defence, and are somewhat familiar with the question of colonial defence. As popularly understood, these two questions have very contracted meanings: the one signifying the protection of the British Islands, and the other the guarding of some particular colonial border. To our thinking, however, national defence can no more be considered an abstract question than colonial defence can be regarded as connected only with the defence of this or of that British colony or dependency. Imperial defence may be said to embrace the former two, as those terms are generally applied. Now, we regard Imperial defence as an obligation binding upon the nation at large."—*Port Elizabeth Telegraph*, May 23rd, 1874.

The military policy has been to disarm the giant in order to arm the dwarf.

I must, however, here observe that I do not argue against the pressing necessity which existed for defending the Imperial base of operations by withdrawing the insufficient garrisons formerly maintained in the colonial outposts; on the contrary, I was one of the first to advocate the withdrawal of the few regular troops quartered in certain colonies and possessions,* as a necessary part of a scheme of Imperial defence; but that scheme did not propose to leave the question of the defence of our colonies and possessions in the air, as has been done. What appears objectionable in the military policy pursued is, that it has been confined to the narrow limits of the defence of the Imperial base, to the exclusion of all considerations for the safety of our Imperial communications, the security of our colonies, and the maintenance of our power in distant possessions.

I therefore venture to assert that before these troops were withdrawn, before the question of military re-organization was practically dealt with, it was the duty of statesmen to cast their eyes beyond the shores of "Happy England," to look beyond the "streak of silver sea," and to face this truth, viz., that the security of the United Kingdom against invasion is but a part of the

* For the purpose of concentrating them at certain strategic and Imperial positions.

great question of "National Defence." It is now nearly five years since, at the Royal United Service Institution,* I endeavoured to draw attention to this fact, in these words:—"The defence of the United Kingdom against invasion is an object of primary importance, but to suppose that this is the one thing needful in the matter of national defence, is a grievous error. We are bound to look to the general welfare of the Empire.† The sources of

* 'Lectures on the Distribution of our War Forces,' 1869.

† **West Indies.**—"The future relations of England and her colonies have a bearing on the question of colonial defence of more practical importance than any other consideration. They will be found to afford grounds for more satisfaction and encouragement than is derived from the history of the past. England has thriven by her colonies, and may reasonably expect to continue to thrive by them in a greater degree in proportion to the development of their resources. Her colonies are at all times, in peace or war, her best allies."—*The West Indian*, April 10th, 1874.

Australia.—"The withdrawal of the regular troops from outlying and detached portions of the British Colonial Empire does not, we are happy to observe, meet with any denunciation in this paper. The policy of concentration has indeed been accepted with almost unanimous concurrence, and in the case of what was thought to be the most valuable portion of the British Colonial Empire, it has called forth such an encouraging demonstration of military capacity for organization, that no politician of any established reputation would dream of reverting to the principle of garrisoning the colonies with men drawn from any other source than the colonies themselves. It is now admitted on all hands that they are at least as capable of protecting themselves as the people of the United Kingdom are. But we take it that it was the purport of Captain Colomb to show that the defence of what is called the British Empire involves world-wide considerations, which cannot be narrowed to the confines of the islands separated from the continent of Europe by the British Channel and the German Ocean. The maintenance of what he calls the Imperial main lines of communication is essential to the successful defence of the Empire, and in effect he invites the colonies to say how they would propose to assist one another in asserting the maritime supremacy of the British

our greatness are the possession of India, and our commercial prosperity. Our commercial prosperity is in direct proportion to the freedom with which we can carry on trade with our colonies and other countries. Commerce is in fact the link that binds together the several interests of the scattered territories comprising the Empire. . . . Bearing this in mind, let us suppose that the view which limits national defence to the protection of Great Britain and Ireland against invasion be practically adopted, and that the whole resources of the country have been wholly and exclusively directed to rendering the *soil* of the British Isles secure, and that this object has been fully attained, what would our position be in time of aggressive war on the part of one or more great powers? Does it not stand to reason that, as the object of all aggressive war is either to acquire territory, or to weaken, if not destroy, the power of the nation against which war is made, the easiest and the safest mode is adopted to carry out these objects: under the circumstances we have supposed, therefore, an enemy would naturally confine his efforts to destroying our commerce and our power in

Empire, for that is really what it amounts to."—*Brisbane Courier*, June 11th, 1874.

South Africa.—" It is cheering, after the narrow and selfish views which have been of late years, not only unblushingly advocated, but almost established as political axioms in England, to hear Englishmen once again extending their sympathies, so long contracted within the silver streak; once more recognizing the fact of a British Empire; once more awake to the principle of union, as absolutely necessary for defence."—*The Times of Natal*, June 24th, 1874.

India, leaving the British Isles to watch his proceeding with impotent dismay."

If the heart and citadel of the Empire is alone protected, will it " surprise us to hear " that, when the Empire is attacked, our enemy prefers cutting our unprotected communications and appropriating our undefended colonies and possessions, to a direct assault upon a " small island bristling with bayonets " ? *

* **Australia.**—" The question of colonial defences is one which has at various times, when there were rumours of wars, occupied a good deal of attention in England, but it has never yet been considered of sufficient importance, or urgency, to require being dealt with in a systematic manner. When Canada a few years ago was threatened with invasion, the Government of the day expressed its intention, if need were, to defend that dependency with its last man and its last ship; and no doubt, had the occasion arisen, thousands of British soldiers and millions of British money would have been poured across the Atlantic. At about the same period all the small military detachments which had previously been stationed in the Australian colonies were withdrawn, and we were, in effect, told that we must ourselves provide for the defence of our ' hearths and homes.' Some of our neighbours set to work, after a fashion, to prepare to receive an enemy: New South Wales did a little in the way of fortification at Sydney, as did Victoria at Port Phillip Heads, Sandridge, and Williamstown ; and the latter-named colony went so far as to invest in a turret-ship. As a portion of a well-devised scheme, each and all of these works would probably prove effective ; isolated as they are, at the most they could but protect a very limited area. The thing, to be successful, must be treated in a comprehensive way; and that, unfortunately, has not hitherto been the case. Except in conjunction with the Imperial naval and military forces, acting upon some pre-arranged plan, any puny efforts the colonies might individually make would be comparatively futile."—*Queensland Times*, June 4th, 1874.

New Zealand.—" This is the forcible point in Captain Colomb's excellent paper, and it is one which comes home very closely to every colonist."—*The Cornwall Chronicle*, June 22nd, 1874.

Malta.—" And if England is to maintain that position among the European nations which she has so deservedly earned, she must be prepared to assert that position much sooner, perhaps, than may be generally expected. That, when the hour of trial and of danger arrives,

In the celebrated article in the *Edinburgh Review* it is written: "Steam applied to navigation has done at least as much for a defending as for an invading Power; even the stores of coals needed for marine locomotion are principally ours; and while by the aid of this powerful agent the ships of both nations may scour the coasts with favourable weather at from twelve to fifteen or sixteen miles an hour, the railways which gird the land, to say nothing of the telegraphs, may in all weathers carry the armies which are to guard it and their *matériel* from point to point at twenty, thirty, or forty." *

Now these are the utterances of a master mind, but it is passing strange that it never seems to have occurred to the writer that we cannot limit the field of operations of an opposing fleet. If our enemy's fleets can scour the coasts of "Happy England" at from twelve to fifteen or sixteen miles an hour, they can scour the coasts of "Unhappy Colonies and Possessions" at the same

she may be found strong and invulnerable in all points, is a consummation which all her sons cannot but be most anxious to promote."—*Public Opinion*, Malta, April 1st, 1874.

Canada.—"We still require political consideration, and the infusion into the councils of the Empire of an element that will always enlarge the political idea, and teach the English people that its defence means something more than the 'hedgerows' of the United Kingdom. Speaking for ourselves, we want the recognition of the principle that there is no difference in the Imperial policy between the County of Middlesex in England, and the County of Middlesex in the Dominion of Canada."—*The Volunteer Review*, Canada, January 27th, 1874.

* 'Germany, France and England.' By the Right Hon. W. E. Gladstone. *Edinburgh Review*, 1870.

rate, where their operations will not be hampered by the presence of any army at all. Even the stores of coal needed for marine locomotion, " though principally ours," are conveniently situated at commanding points along the Imperial roads, and, by being for the most part totally neglected and undefended, afford a guarantee that the enemy's fleets shall not be inconvenienced by want of fuel in a raid upon " our vast Colonial empire, our extended commerce, and interests in *any* part of the globe."

It is said that a certain bird when hard pressed in its flight buries its head in the sand, and finds imaginary security because it ceases to see the near approach of danger; and the present policy pursued by this country in the matter of defence appears to me to be somewhat analogous. Our Imperial Eagle, whose wings cover the seas, buries her head in the sands of the defended shores of England, and blinding her vision of danger with a few men, guns, volunteer reviews, and autumn manœuvres, her statesmen bid her believe that she is safe!

This is one side of the picture; let us glance briefly at the other. It is not many years ago since our defensive measures were based upon an exactly opposite principle, and one equally dangerous to the safety of our Empire. Our armies and our fleets were scattered indiscriminately over the face of the globe, while the United Kingdom (the Imperial base of operations) was left destitute of any power of resistance. All our war force was exhausted on means for the direct defence of our colonies and distant possessions, to the exclusion of all considerations relative to the security of the Imperial base.*

The defenceless state of the British Islands at the time of which I speak, can best be pictured by

* **Australia.**—"That there has been a change of policy in respect to the disposition of the British forces, everybody knows, and few regret. The scattered armies were of small account after all. Any little hubbub over the determination to concentrate rather than distribute the Imperial forces has disappeared, and many wonder why so much fuss was made about so little. A 'pressing necessity' did exist for defending 'the Imperial base of operations' by withdrawing the insufficient garrisons formerly maintained on the colonial outposts; for, with slight exception, they were needless, expensive, and happily got rid of. To the exception we shall recur. Meantime it may be observed that the colonies are quite satisfied with their own little armies. They will be able to do all the work that is required of them. The New South Wales soldiers are men who literally have an interest in defending their homes, for the guerdon of their service and efficiency is a portion of the land they occupy. This material stimulus to patriotism is, however, unnecessary, for in a time of imminent peril our citizen army would bravely take the field."—*Sydney Morning Herald*, June 8th, 1874.

New Zealand.—"This, however, would be carrying the self-reliant policy to an absurdity. By that policy we do not understand that England is to leave any portion of her territory to bear the full brunt of an enemy's attack, but only that each district is to provide all the means in its power to resist invasion, and England will do the rest. Surely the most ardent advocate of self-reliance would not argue that, in the event of the United States concentrating all their strength in an attack upon the West Indies, Great Britain should refrain from sending a soldier or sailor to their defence! Supposing England and the United States were at war, and the latter made an attack upon Jamaica with all their military power, it is evident that the other parts of the British Empire would, for the time, be relieved from the danger of attack, and thus the concentrated assault could be met by a concentrated defence."—*Wanganui Chronicle*, June 5th, 1874.

recalling the concluding words of the celebrated letter of the Duke of Wellington, in which he showed the ease with which these islands could be carried by assault: " I am bordering on seventy-seven years passed in honour. I hope that the Almighty may protect me from being a witness of the tragedy, which I cannot persuade my contemporaries to take measures to avert." We were then as oblivious to the truth that the capture of the citadel involved the downfall of the Empire as we are now blind to the fact that the security of that citadel is no guarantee for the safety of *fifty-nine-sixtieths* of British territory, or for the protection of the lives and properties of *six-sevenths* of Her Majesty's subjects.

In avoiding Scylla we have encountered Charybdis. Where, then, is the true channel through which the Empire may safely pass, defying attack ? Many may think, with the Government of the day, that this question may be solved by saying to our colonies and possessions—Arm yourselves; it is every man's duty to defend his hearth and home. Do as we have done in England, raise volunteers, create what military forces you please, do as we have done, and our Empire is safe! Now, let us consider whether this be a true solution of the problem. In the first place, it is not possible to lay down a general rule of self-reliance and self-defence applicable to all colonies and possessions alike. The power of resistance of each fragment of the Empire can only be measured by a comparison between its population, its geographical position, and natural defensive advantages, and those of its possible enemy. It is simply ridiculous to tell any one of our West Indian islands to be self-reliant, and to trust to its citizens to resist the war power of the United States. If this general rule is the basis of our plan of Imperial defence, and is to be applied, it means in plain English that in the unhappy event of a rupture with America, we offer that nation peaceable and quiet possession of 100,000 square miles of territory, and make over the lives and properties of $1\frac{1}{4}$ million of British subjects.

I fear it would not be difficult to find what are termed "advanced thinkers" in the country—nay, in Parliament, and seated on Government benches —who would not think this a very great national calamity. Possibly such persons might argue that the United States would allow the money value of these territories as a set-off in the final balance-sheet of American claims of indemnity for expenses caused by war. It is therefore necessary to observe that the loss of the West Indies affects the safety of Canada. First, by increasing the resources of the United States; secondly, by securing to that power the command of the Western Atlantic—thus rendering it impossible for Imperial forces to create a diversion in favour of Canada, in the hour of trial, by blockade and attack on the southern and eastern shores of America.*

It follows, therefore, that the general and indiscriminate application of the policy of fragmentary self-reliance and self-defence, though possible to Canada as a direct means of frontier defence—besides involving the loss of other possessions—is

---

* **West Indies.**—"It is well for us there is the prospect of the continuance of peaceful and friendly relations between Great Britain and the other nations of the world for a series of years, during which the colonies will have time to grow to maturity and to strengthen themselves by drawing closer the bonds of union. The West Indies form an important link in the chain of communication between those situated on the shores of the North and South Atlantic, and even between the Australian colonies and England, the chief trade being carried on round the capes. It is in the common interest of all that this link of the chain should not be allowed to drop out or to be broken, for the question of colonial defence must be regarded as a whole, and not in parts; not in respect of any particular colony, or of the defence of England, Scotland, and Ireland, and the command of the Channel only, but of all the colonies, which are integral parts of the Empire, and keeping open the communications between them across the seas. Towards this union and consolidation of interests nothing avails more than the sense of the mutual advantages derived from the alliance by all the parties to it. What these are may be seen in one—in India, where the British name is a tower of strength, a talisman against internal dissension and jealousies, as well as against foreign aggression. The flag of England guarantees the safety of all those who cross the seas, while it secures peace and good government everywhere. The colonies enjoy the benefits of the equal laws and free institutions of the mother country. Each has its own local administration, making its own laws, and raising and appropriating its own revenues, without derogation from the dignity and prerogatives of the British Crown. So long as the sense of these mutual advantages prevails in the colonies, that loyal attachment which they have always shown towards the mother country, and none more so than the West Indies, will continue to exist, and continue to be the strongest assurance of their trust in England,—the ground on which they look for her protection in the hour of danger."—*West Indian*, April 7th, 1874.

the most certain method of ensuring she shall be left in her struggle unaided and alone.

Similar arguments apply with equal force to other colonies and possessions elsewhere; but as it is impossible to deal with this great question in a short paper, I think I have said enough to show that this general rule of "self-reliance" fails to solve the problem of Imperial Defence. The question therefore remains—What are the general principles on which the defence of the Empire must be based?*

Before we can give a reply worthy of the name, it is essential that we should understand what is the Empire, and what is vital to its existence. Speaking generally of its geographical position, it consists of ten groups of territory separated by long sea-distances. The British Islands, British North America, the West Indies,

---

* Australia.—"But in times of peace, far removed from the din of battle and the tumult of opinion, it is well to consider dispassionately the position we occupy, and how we would be situated in the event of war. Besides, it is only in such times that we can fully realize the best and the worst of existing policies and systems, and alter or amend them in accordance with the dictates of prudence and the fullest experience. The greatest battles of late years were battles fought on clearly-defined principles and the amplest information. It is well known that the Germans, in anticipation of the bitter revival of the Rhine question, made France a special study, and found good means to draw from her in peaceful years the secret of her overthrow. Nowadays, as ever, to be warned is to be forearmed; and further, to test and reflect on the policy we espouse is to make us more fit to grapple with any difficulty that may arise. European complications may ere long attract our notice, without touching us home in the smallest degree; but, meantime, it is as well to look in the face aught that might endanger us then."—*Sydney Morning Herald*, June 8th, 1874.

the West Coast of Africa, the Cape, the Mauritius, Australasia, Hong Kong, the Straits Settlements, and India.

This is a rough sketch of the ground to be defended. Now, to quote from a work by Sir C. Pasley, written in 1808,* "The strength of an empire composed of several islands or possessions, divided from each other by the sea, will be further modified by the geographical position of its respective parts. The strength of an empire of any kind, whether insular or continental, will be greater or less, with equal resources, in proportion to the facility with which its several parts can afford each other mutual assistance when attacked, and to the difficulty which an enemy may find in supplying and supporting his invading force." †

This able exposition of a great military truth brings to light two great principles:—

1. That it is of vital importance that the safety of the Imperial communications be secured.

2. That it is essential to the military strength of the Empire that forces created or existing for the defence of one portion be not so constituted as to preclude the possibility of using them in the defence of another.

If the Imperial communications are not secured,

---

* 'The Military Policy and Institutions of the British Empire.'

† **New Zealand.**—"Although this had no reference to the Australias, and was written as far back as 1808, no stronger argument could be adduced in the present day in favour of Colonial Federation."—*Cornwall Chronicle*, June 22nd, 1874.

our enemy can make it *physically* impossible for the several parts to afford "mutual assistance when attacked." On the other hand, although they may be tolerably safe, if the military forces of each part are by law so constituted as to preclude the power of moving them to another, we ourselves render it a *moral* impossibility for the several parts to afford "mutual assistance when attacked." In the one case the enemy cripples the necessary power of concentration; in the other we save him the trouble by doing it ourselves. What then becomes of the military value of forces constituted as our militia and volunteers are, at home or in the colonies, when weighed in the Imperial scales?

If the Empire is to be defended at all we must apply, on a large scale, the ordinary and common military principle applicable to the defence of all territory, large or small.

The fundamental principle is briefly this. The success of all operations of war, whether defensive or offensive, depends upon the disposition of force in such a manner as will best secure the base of operations, and ensure safety and freedom of communication. It is useless to do one without the other, for in the one case neglect of the rule must lead to a "lock-out," in the other the "lock-up" of military force. Our former disposition of our force risked the "lock-out" of military force by rendering the capture of the base possible: our present plan endangers, nay courts, the "lock-up" of military force at the base by leaving our communications exposed, and outposts undefended.*

In the late war we saw first of all an attack upon the advanced positions on the lines of communication; next the cutting of the lines of communication; and lastly, as an inevitable consequence, Paris fell.

The United Kingdom is our Imperial base. The Imperial main lines of communication are :—

1. To British North America across the North Atlantic.
2. To the West Indies.

---

* **Australia.**—The well-drilled Voluntary force, auxiliary to a properly-recruited and powerful regular Army, encircled, too, by the finest and strongest Navy in the world, may dispel any fears we might foolishly entertain regarding the safety of our island home. But it is not so with the rest of the Empire. The centre, the citadel, is secure, but the outposts are not invulnerable. The scattered immensity of our Empire leaves it peculiarly open and liable to attack, unless measures are concerted and carried out for its due and full protection. The altered policy of the Imperial Government renders this fact doubly significant and urgent. When the violation of solemn treaties, which were bonds written in blood, is permitted or connived at, and our "moral" influence is the only supreme influence we can boast, if indeed it is worth bragging about, it is high time to scan the political horizon and watch for the black clouds that may loom even over the Euxine. At a time, too, when a faithful ally and the control of a highway to some of our richest lands are surrendered voluntarily, we may be chary of trusting hasty politicians or incautious and over-sympathetic statesmen. It is blazoned on our patriotic shield that the sun never sets on our Empire, and that very truth it is which proclaims to us the dangers our vast possessions, wealth, and commerce entail on us. Everywhere our flag flies the honour of England is at stake, and a shock or injury to any member of the Empire is felt at the remotest extremity."—*Sydney Morning Herald,* June 8th, 1874.

3. To India, China, and Australasia by the Mediterranean.
4. To India, China, and Australasia round the Cape.
5. From Australasia and the Pacific round Cape Horn.

The Imperial base can be reduced in two ways:—

1. By direct assault : invasion.
2. By indirect means : investment.

It is curious—I trust I may be forgiven for saying it—that while the possibility of invasion is not generally disputed, I believe I happen to be the only individual who believes in investment; at least I know of no other who has for eight years tried to force on public attention the fact that the certainty of investment, partial or complete, follows the *possibility* of invasion as surely as night follows day.

Consider for one moment on what the presumption of possible invasion rests. It rests on this—the loss, temporary or permanent, of the command of the waters surrounding the British Islands. But remember that the lines of communication *all* radiate from these waters; the loss, therefore, of our command *here* cuts every one of the Imperial lines; and what is this, *but* investment?

The statesman who could, in a magazine, speak complacently of an opposing force " scouring our coasts at twelve, fifteen, or sixteen miles an hour," must surely have forgotten that the heart of the Empire thus cut off from its sources of supply must cease to beat.* Hardly a mile could be so traversed in triumphant defiance without injury, in a greater or less degree, to some artery or nerve, producing in some far-off member of the body politic of the Empire results more or less disastrous. It might be but a nervous tremor produced by a temporary disarrangement of the free course of trade, or it might be paralysis caused by a prolonged interruption of the vital powers of communication. The question of results is but a question of time.

As regards the safety of communications, it must be borne in mind that the greatest danger to which they can be exposed is that which threatens the greatest number at one and the same time. Geographically speaking, this can only happen at the point of convergence or radiation, which in our case is the Channel.

The Royal Commission of 1859 discarded the Channel Fleet as a first line of defence against invasion, because " Were an undue proportion of our fleet tied to the Channel " our enemy's " would be proportionably set free, to the great danger of

---

* **Australia.**—" The question of Colonial Defences is, of course, paramount with us."—*Sydney Morning Herald*, June 8th, 1874.

Canada.—" Naturally Englishmen, in whatever part of the British Empire they may be placed, feel they are as fully entitled to the protecting *ægis* of the Mother Country as if living in their native land. . . . True defence must be Imperial and not national."—*British Colonist*, Victoria, B.C., February 20th, 1877.

our colonies and to the injury of a commerce which becomes of more vital importance with every step of national progress." But I desire to observe that, though it may not be our first line of defence against invasion, it is our first line of defence against investment, and, further, the front of our first line of colonial defence. Of what avail is it if our colonies, though protected in their own immediate neighbourhood, are "locked-out" from the mother country by a force in the Channel, against which we are unable to contend? Of what use is it protecting our commerce on distant seas if it is to be destroyed within sight of the shores of England? Surely, in reckoning up our means of defence, we should not forget that if our enemy confines his operations to an attack on our communications, and we are unprepared to resist it, the forces we have created for the special purpose of repelling invasion will be after all but a harmless host of spectators of a ruin they are powerless to avert.

I do not for a moment underrate the immense importance and absolute necessity of being prepared to render invasion impossible by purely military forces. If we are not so prepared we stake the fate of the Empire on, perhaps, a single naval engagement. A temporary reverse at sea might (by the enemy following up his advantage) be converted into final defeat on land, resulting in a total overthrow of all further power of resistance. It is necessary for the *safety of the Channel* that invasion be efficiently guarded against, so that should our home fleet be temporarily disabled we may, under cover of our army, prepare and strengthen it to regain lost ground, and renew the struggle for that which is essential to our life as a nation, and our existence as an empire—the command of the waters of the United Kingdom.

We are all so keenly alive to the necessity of rendering invasion impossible, that this part of the subject may now be dismissed. I may also pass from the front of the first line of colonial defence with the remark, that the fleet required to maintain it must not be confused nor mixed up with the cruising force necessary for the safety of the distant lines of communication. To hold our supremacy of the Channel we require a force composed of vessels adapted to the combined action of fleets, and of a strength equal to that which may possibly be brought against it. This remark also applies to the protection of the line of communication passing through the Mediterranean. But on more distant seas, for the protection of such lines, a special class of cruisers, capable of keeping at sea for long periods of time, is required; the strength of this patrolling force on each line being in proportion to the value of the line, and to the force against which it may have to contend. The fleets necessary for the safety of the Channel and Mediterranean are not adapted to the protection of distant lines, nor are the vessels suited to the defence of those lines of any value as a reserve force to be called in to aid in the defence of the Channel and Mediterranean.

But the defence of our communications is not secured by the mere presence of sufficient naval force at home or in the Mediterranean; for as there are two modes of attack on the United Kingdom, so there are two ways in which our lines of communication may be destroyed. 1st. By direct attack on the point of convergence. 2nd. By a variety of attacks on one or more lines at points far removed from the place where they all meet.*
Assuming provision for meeting the first to have

---

* **Australia.**—"Difficulties that seemed insurmountable have been in two recent instances expeditiously and triumphantly overcome. The story of Hannibal almost pales before our campaign in Abyssinia; and the Ashantee war is a glorious proof of England's rapid power of enforcing her authority and displaying her ability to transport troops to far-off countries. But the dangers that would menace us could only arise from wars of a different kind; yet even then, we repeat, England could readily stretch out her arm to aid her colonial armies. For the reasons stated, we do not agree with Captain Colomb when he ventures to speak lightly of 'the general rule of self-reliance.' Why, that is the inspiring rule of our colonies, the very genius of a self-made people. And if the general rule of self-reliance 'fails to solve the problem of Imperial defence,' it nevertheless goes far towards its solution.

"But the question bears an altered complexion when we come to look at the vulnerability of the Empire along the lines of communication. It is essential to our commercial prosperity that our ships should sail the ocean unmolested, and that our great southern and eastern marts and cities should be secured from attack. 'Commerce is, in fact, the link that binds together the several interests of the scattered territories comprising the Empire.' The destruction of her commerce would be the ruin of Britain. She must still rule the wave, and inspire confidence in those who trust their argosies to her powerful care. And no fear of attack or investment will ever make us quake so long as we know that England can protect her ships, for she can then intercept an enemy's fleet."—*Sydney Morning Herald*, June 8th, 1874.

been made, I will now deal with the means to be adopted to meet this other mode of attack; and this is the most interesting portion of my subject.

(Communications, whether sea or land, whether long or short, *can only be secured by a firm grasp of the points which command them.*) The greater the extent of the line, the greater is the number of defended points necessary for its safety. In order to cut a line of communication, the first thing to be done is to seize the point which commands it,* and in defending a line the point which commands it is the last to surrender. Such points are the minor bases of operation of forces acting in defence of the line. The relative importance of such points to the line, and to each other, can only be estimated by the circumstances of their geographical position and their distance from the main base from which the line springs.

There is this difference, however, between the defence of sea as compared with land communications. Naturally in the second, a purely military force only is required, but in the case of sea lines the employment of a purely military as well as a purely naval force is necessary. The navy furnishes the patrolling or skirmishing force, while the army secures to it its bases or arsenals. To leave the naval force responsible for the protection of its

---

* **New Zealand.**—"... Extreme danger would put the whole of the Empire on its metal, nor do we fear that the result would be less favourable to England than similar perilous crises have been."—*Cornwall Chronicle*, June 5th, 1874.

base would be to tie its hands. It would be "using the fleet to maintain its arsenals, instead of the arsenals to maintain the fleet."* Some years ago a governor of an eastern colony proposed to leave such places almost exclusively to naval protection, and the late Sir John Burgoyne thus speaks of the value of the proposition: " Under the system proposed, a small squadron, with 3000 or 4000 troops, in eastern seas in time of war, would take the Mauritius and Hong Kong, and destroy the naval arsenal and means at Trincomalee, if it did not capture the whole island of Ceylon." †

The force thus alluded to might be Russian or that of some other power. In any case, how would the loss of Ceylon affect our military position in India? Is it likely that aggression would stop there? Might it not gather strength, and might not Ceylon be a convenient base of operation for an attack on Australasia? If, therefore, we trust the protection of our lines exclusively to a purely naval force, by imposing on our fleets the defence of the points which command them, we risk, nay, we court a general attack, not on England, not on the Channel, but on " our vast Colonial Empire, our extended commerce, and interest in every quarter of the globe." ‡

* *Vide* Defence Commission Report, 1859.
† See Appendix to ' Life of Field-Marshal Sir J. Burgoyne.
‡ **Hong Kong.**—" That this is not an exaggeration of the danger that would be incurred will be readily believed from the fact that when the last great war broke out on the Continent, and it was rumoured that England would be involved in it, the question as to the safety of Hong Kong was discussed here with anxiety, as, small though this colony is, it would be a most important blow to British prestige in the

It is now time to ask what are these points? and, in an attempt to reply, I will take each line separately:—

1. The line to Canada. The only point here is a terminal one—it is Halifax.

2. To the West Indies. Here we have Bermuda, the Bahamas, Jamaica and Antigua. The strategic value of Bermuda is in some degree understood. The military value of the Bahamas was fixed by Sir John Burgoyne.* Jamaica, from its central position and capacious harbour, is of considerable importance. I add Antigua for two reasons—(1) because Jamaica is far too leeward to

whole of China, and as a necessary consequence also in India, were it captured even for a short period by a foreign power; and the evil effects which would be thus produced might be an object in time of war. In Hong Kong a regiment is stationed, and there are usually a fair number of men-of-war on the station; but, if hostilities broke out at home, the naval forces might possibly be reduced even further than they have been by the retrenching policy of the Government of late years, and the danger above indicated be incurred. This colony pays a military contribution of 20,000l., which has not unjustly been objected to, because the forces are stationed here as much in the general interest of Great Britain in China as in those of Hong Kong, and the amount is very heavy for so small a colony. Captain Colomb suggests that a general and enlarged scheme for the defence of the sea-communications of the Empire can only be made by the colonies cooperating, and one of the first things that would have to be done would be to adjust the contributions from the different colonies upon a well-considered and equitable basis. At present, these contributions are levied capriciously, and frequently cause much discontent; but there can be little doubt that the colonies for the most part would willingly contribute towards the general defence of the Empire, if, in return, they had some voice in the government; and it would be a good adjunct towards the consummation of such a policy as Captain Colomb agitates that some measures for the representation of the colonies in the Imperial Parliament were taken."—*The Daily Press*, Hong Kong, May 1, 1874.

* See Appendix to 'Life of Field-Marshal Sir J. Burgoyne.'

be of value as a coaling station or arsenal for cruisers acting in the defence of communications to the Eastern Islands; such vessels would burn a great quantity of fuel in steaming up to their station from Jamaica against the trades; (2) vessels bound for the greater Antilles and Gulf of Mexico generally pass between Antigua and Guadeloupe.

3. To India, the East, and Australasia, by the Mediterranean. The points here are Gibraltar, Malta,* Aden, Bombay, Cape Comorin,† and King George's Sound on the main line, with Trin-

* **Malta.**—" There can be no doubt that the Imperial Government is fully alive to the great importance of Malta as a naval and military station: the improvements recently carried out in its armament and the additional works of defence which are even now being constructed, appear to have rendered the island absolutely impregnable. On the other hand, are the warlike stores and the war material on the spot, sufficient to meet the emergencies contemplated by Captain Colomb, and which alone can justify the annual expenditure of so much treasure? And what is of still greater importance, is the number of men permanently stationed here sufficient to man even the most important works of defence? Where could be found a safer or better defended depôt for both men and war material to be used, not only in defending the island, but also to be dispatched, at the shortest notice, to India and the other distant dependencies of the Crown? Is the dock accommodation sufficient to repair and refit such ships as may be disabled in an engagement at so great a distance from England? And what about the coal depôts? These are all considerations which have no doubt occurred to the able naval and military commanders on the station; though they may have remained unheeded by the Central Government, especially under the rigid economy preached by the late Administration."
—*Public Opinion*, Malta, April 1, 1874.

† Although there is not now any harbour of importance at Cape Comorin, those who have read the paper on "Indian Harbours" by General Sir A. Cotton, will understand the strategic importance of the position, and the possibility of creating a harbour at "Colachul" in its vicinity.

comalee, Singapore, and Hong Kong on its northern branch.

Of all the Imperial roads this is the most difficult to defend, owing to its want of continuity. The most commanding position—the Isthmus of Suez—is not in our possession. Here our line can be most easily cut, and here we have least power to prevent the contingency. So long as the canal is neutral or in the hands of a neutral power, so long is it at the disposal of friend and foe alike. Were it in the hands of our enemies, it is only open to them and not to us. To make this line safe, the occupation by military force of the Isthmus might, under certain conditions, be a necessity. Are we prepared for that?

Supposing it to be neutral, it must be remembered that if purely naval power cannot be entirely relied on for the local protection of our outposts, neither can it be relied on to prevent the entry into the Nile of vessels of our enemy, and once there they would have the whole of our Eastern possessions at their mercy, unless we have a force sufficient to blockade the Red Sea. But as the necessity for the existence of such a force rests on the possibility of our direct communications being cut somewhere between the Red Sea and the English Channel, it is important to consider how our fleets in the East could exist, without adequate means of supply and repair, independent of our home resources.

Such considerations as these point to the absolute necessity of having a commanding and strongly-defended great naval arsenal in the Eastern hemisphere. Here we might have ships and stores in reserve; here should be the great base of naval operations in peace and war for all our Eastern fleets. Is it safe to assume that the resources of Portsmouth, Chatham, and Plymouth would be equal to the task of supplying our war fleets throughout the world at such time with ships, stores, and means of repair? Can we dream of private firms during maritime war taking contracts to maintain in a state of efficiency war fleets 6000 and 10,000 miles off?*

With the development of the resources of India, Australia, New Zealand, and a host of smaller possessions, the necessity for securing their roads increases; so also increases the power of providing

* **Australia.**—"These are precisely the considerations which affect the outlying portions of the Empire. Secure and unbroken communication with Britain is essential to the safety of the Empire, and the means requisite to ensure this are decidedly within our reach. The first condition is the existence of a strong army for home defence; the second, the existence of a sufficient force in each of the most exposed outposts; the third, the existence of additional forces ready to be moved if required to other distant possessions; and the fourth, the existence of a fleet to protect the Imperial centre, to guard our commerce, and to transport the necessary troops on emergency. England must ever have an army of occupation in India, and garrisons in her foreign dependencies, and 'towers along the steep.' Her sentry-boxes along the ocean highway must never be vacant, nor her harbours of refuge neglected. But this is quite a different thing from planting a standing army in thoroughly English colonies. Besides, the troops required to strengthen her valuable posts, and garrison her strategic points, may be spared in time of peace from the regular army, and kept as cheaply on such foreign service."—*Sydney Morning Herald*, June 8th, 1874.

and supporting adequate means of defence.* With a Russian sea-board on the one hand, and an American sea-board on the other, it cannot be said that by their remoteness from us they are removed from danger of attack: nor must it be forgotten that the very fact of their distance from us adds to our difficulties in defending them, unless by a judicious combination of Imperial resources—to which India should contribute a large proportion—we render the fleets for their defence independent to a large extent of home support.

If naval protection without military protection be productive of danger to the Empire, great disaster may also be expected to result from attempting to hold distant possessions by military force, if that force might be completely isolated and locked out from its sources of supply and reserves for want of the naval protection of its communication with the Imperial base. If it be asked what we have done to guard against the possible isolation of our army in India? the reply is, we have abolished the Indian navy and substituted nothing in its place! Though India supports the army necessary for its safety, it contributes nothing † towards a fleet for the protection and security of the communications of the army, without which it cannot exist.

* The total value of exports and imports of India, Ceylon, and Australasia is about four-fifths of the total value of exports and imports of the United States.

† The contribution from the Indian Government, on account of the expense of a fleet on Indian stations, is practically nothing.

Two circumstances have lately occurred to threaten our command of this direct route—the opening of the Suez Canal, and the removal of the restrictions placed upon Russian power in the Euxine. We agreed to the latter on *moral* grounds. But if on moral grounds we have practically shown our sympathy with the desire of Russia to accumulate physical force in the Black Sea, we should extend our sympathy to India and our Eastern colonies, and be careful that it takes an equally practical form, by the creation of a naval arsenal adapted to the probable requirement of the defence of their communications: thus balancing the power of resistance * with the increased power of aggres-

* **New Zealand.**—" Of course, Canada and the West Indies occupy a very different military position to the Australias, but what strikes colonists in this part of the world is their exposure to sudden raids upon their shipping and seaport towns. It would be a most difficult task for any foreign power to invade Australia or New Zealand, and even if an invading force effected a landing, its surrender or re-embarkation would very soon take place. But light armed cruisers might do us enormous damage by picking up colonial merchantmen and levying contributions upon our seaports. There is not a seaport town in New Zealand which is protected against such a visitation. Not a torpedo has been sunk in one of our harbours, or a heavy gun planted to command them. Yet there are plenty of trained artillerymen in New Zealand, and sums of money have been spent upon 'Defence Purposes' which would have furnished every town of the colony with two or three guns of the heaviest calibre, whose presence would be quite enough to deter any vessel of the 'Alabama' class from dropping in at Auckland or Wellington some fine morning and asking for a donation of 100,000*l.*, with the certainty of getting it. The subject has been discussed by secret committees of the General Assembly, and been reported upon to the Government by an experienced engineer officer; but nothing has been done. The danger is not visible, and procrastination is so easy. The Australian colonies are little better in this respect, although Victoria has done something for the protection of Melbourne. But

sion which our "moral sympathy" has so generously provided.

To attempt to determine the exact site for such a reserve naval arsenal for the Eastern portion of the Empire would be beyond the scope of this paper, but considerations respecting climate, and its effects on stores, &c., point to some port of Australia,* as best adapted for the purpose. The

---

there is one important part of the military defence of these colonies which has been entirely neglected, and that is the protection of our coal depôts. To the necessity of protecting the coaling stations of the Empire, Captain Colomb draws special attention, and the force of his reasoning is obvious now that sailing war-vessels are obsolete. The grand coaling station in the Southern hemisphere is Newcastle N.S.W., and that town ought unquestionably to be fortified. At present, we believe it is just as defenceless as the city of Wellington."—*Wanganui Chronicle*, June 5th, 1874.

* **Australia.**—" The suggestion is feasible and practicable, and, next to the strategic stationing of our ships, demands earnest and serious attention. Indeed, the one thing depends on the other. A large, scattered, defensive steam fleet requires repairing, and ammunition as well as coal; and the erection of depôts is not more essential than the construction of an arsenal. The outlay would doubtless be great, but even in times of peace the docks might be profitably used for the Government advantage. Wherever such an arsenal might be situated, whether in Bombay or in Australia, it would, we venture to believe, be a great and invaluable support to our defence."—*Sydney Morning Herald*, June 8th, 1874.

" Among other things, Captain Colomb has suggested an arsenal. He is in doubt whether this necessity ought to be Australian or Indian; but, if anything, his inclination leans towards us, and leaning thus, suggests Sydney. Bombay may easily be defended—so far as Bombay requires to be made secure, and as an Indian outpost it will ever command serious and anxious attention. But to talk of it as the centre of repairing, fitting-up, and coaling in this hemisphere, to speak of it as the Woolwich-Portsmouth away from England, is rank absurdity. The circumstances and conditions are averse to the position. Bombay is ours through force, and is but a portion of our wealthiest dependency. As we said in a previous article, no works of such vital importance should be constructed save among our own people. Fortify, strengthen

strategic importance of Bombay,* however, cannot be overlooked. It must be borne in mind that the appliances, such as docks and machinery for repairs, &c., would be available for our commercial fleets in peace; and hence that Imperial resources expended to provide for the contingency of war, could not be regarded as money thrown away in peace.

4th line : To India and the East, and Australasia, round the Cape. Here the points are Sierra Leone, Ascension, St. Helena, Simon's Bay, the Mauritius, and King George's Sound.

5th line : From Australasia and Vancouver's Island, round Cape Horn. Here we have Sierra Leone, Ascension, the Falkland Islands, and Sydney. These points are, however, valueless for the defence of the line between Vancouver's Island

---

Bombay, if they choose; still the British Government know that it is theirs only so long as their prudent strength is asserted. It is far otherwise with Australia. Here is a loyal people, having the welfare and supremacy of the Empire as much at heart as those who see Her Majesty in London, or welcome her victorious troops from the ends of the earth."
—*Ibid.*, June 15th, 1874.

* India.—" The question as to the military force for the protection of our colonies is far beyond our limits. But if they are to be self-reliant, we should provide them with guns for the armament of their batteries, as also other warlike supplies. We should give the colonies the best arms we can supply them with. We might go further, and give them drill-instructors. We believe we are right in stating that the two monitors stationed at Bombay for the protection of the harbour are too weak in men to be able to work their guns with the proper reserve necessary for a naval action. It is therefore self-evident that the question of colonial defence is not deemed worthy of that consideration which the question merits."— *The Englishman*, Calcutta, April 24th, 1874.

and Australia, but a commanding position for this part of the line has been offered to the Government—the Fiji Islands. It remains to be seen whether the Government accepts the offer. It is a position of great importance from an Imperial strategic point of view. The Hydrographer of the Admiralty thus speaks of it: "The Fijis lie nearly in the direct track from Panama to Sydney, and if a steamer touched at one of them for coal she would only lengthen her voyage about 320 miles, or one day's run, in a distance of 8000 miles. In like manner, in the voyage from Vancouver's Island to Sydney, the touching at Fiji would lengthen the distance 420 miles in a voyage of 7000. An intermediate station between Panama and Sydney will be most desirable—indeed, if the proposed mail route be carried out it is indispensable. In the above statement I have confined myself to answering questions referred to me by the Colonial Office; but, on looking into the subject, I have been much struck by the entire want of Great Britain of any advanced position in the Pacific Ocean. We have valuable possessions on either side, as at Vancouver's Island and Sydney, but not an islet or a rock in the 7000 miles that separate them. We have no island on which to place a coaling station, and where we could ensure fresh supplies."

A comparison between the value of our property passing and repassing in the vicinity of these islands with that of other nations, will show that we have a vastly greater interest in maintaining freedom of communications in that district than any other power. It therefore follows that the military value of the position to any other maritime power is greater when regarded as a means of aggression than as necessary for purposes of defence. But to us its possession is vital as a rallying-point of defence, though of small value as a base for offensive operation. On the principle, therefore, of "defence, not defiance" the military arguments for the annexation of the Fijis should meet with the approval of the Government.*

* "In the year 1874, at the instance of the natives, and in consequence of the earnest request of our Australian fellow-countrymen, we reluctantly consented to accept the cession of the Fiji Islands. As had been foreseen, the revenue fell short of the expenditure, and Parliament had to vote 40,000*l.* in 1875, and 35,000*l.* in 1876, to carry on the government of our new colony. Under these circumstances, Lord Carnarvon wrote to inquire whether our four great Australian colonies would be disposed to contribute 4000*l.* a year each, thus still leaving the lion's share of the burden to the mother country. I confess I regret that not one of the colonies has expressed any readiness to do so. Of course Lord Carnarvon did not press the matter; for as he very truly observed in an excellent circular letter of the 9th July, 1875, it would have been 'obviously undesirable, in a matter where the grace of the act depended upon its being voluntary, and where the amount involved was so small that it would be mainly valuable as proving the readiness of the great colonies to accept their membership in the common duties of the Empire, to put the slightest pressure upon any one of them to make this joint contribution. It was, as I explained in my former dispatch, principally to give trial and effect to the principle of joint action among different members of the Empire in such a case, that I invited co-operation in a matter in which the contributions proposed were so inconsiderable as to make it practically immaterial, except in connection with such a principle, whether the arrangement could at once be carried out.'

This very hasty sketch of the ground to be defended must necessarily be subject to modification and alteration on more accurate and minute survey. It must be regarded only at present as an attempt to apply general principles to the Empire as a whole.*

In the selection of the points the following conditions should be fulfilled:—1. They must be in our possession, and on or near a line of communication. 2. They should possess natural advantages, such as safe and commodious shelter for the war and commercial fleets, easy of access, and capable of defence. 3. They should be as far as possible the natural rendezvous at all times of vessels passing and repassing along the line, and the chief,

"Sir Julius Vogel, the Prime Minister of New Zealand, gave as one reason for his declining the suggestion, 'it is not the business of governments to be liberal,' which is perhaps true, but there is also an opposite course which seems still less appropriate. Sir Julius does not deny that New Zealand felt a great interest in the annexation of Fiji; but he urges that it 'was trifling as compared with the interest which the mother country had in it.'"—'The Imperial Policy of Great Britain,' by Sir John Lubbock.

* **New Zealand.**—"Two of his recommendations forcibly impress a New Zealand colonist. One is, that a naval arsenal should be established for the Eastern portion of the Empire. An Australian port he deems would be best adapted for the purpose; at the same time, the strategic importance of Bombay cannot be overlooked. The other recommendation is, that the Imperial Government should take possession of the Fijis in order to command the line between Australia and Vancouver's Island. The military importance of the Fijis has been urged again and again by the Australian and New Zealand journals; and it may safely be asserted that unless the Imperial Government assumes their sovereignty in time of peace, the first thing the Australian Colonies will have to do for self-protection, upon war breaking out, will be to seize the group, lest it should become the refuge of a host of privateers."—*Wanganui Chronicle*, June 5th, 1874.

if not the only, coaling station of the district they command.

Too much attention cannot be paid to the selection of the coaling stations of the Empire. They should be under our control. Take, for example, the West Indies. The great coaling station in that district—St. Thomas—is not in our possession. The consequence is, that were we engaged in hostilities in that quarter, a large portion of our force would be necessarily employed in the blockade—so far as our enemy is concerned—of this point, and would be so much deducted from the force available and required for other purposes.

It is possible at first sight Sierra Leone and Ascension* may not appear to be of Imperial

---

* **St. Helena.**—" At St. Helena we have had some lessons which, if Captain Colomb's views gain acceptance, may be of value. In the Russian War of 1854-5, and in the American Civil War of 1862-4, we had here at St. Helena illustrations of the value of the island as a point of protection to our trade. Had the Russian frigates in 1854 made a dash at this island and carried it, they could without doubt have held the place for six months at least, and what interruption and damage to our shipping would have ensued may be imagined. The famous cruise of the 'Alabama' in the American War will show what might be done by one single cruiser between the Cape and St. Helena, if there were no force at hand to protect our commerce. . . . Two small islands in the South Atlantic Ocean are both possibly of importance in some contingency—St. Helena and Ascension. In the ordinary course of things it would be imagined these two little Islands should be united under one Government. But no, that is not at all the case. Ascension belongs to the Admiralty. It is not a colony, but a ship; while St. Helena is admitted to the full honours of a British colony and is governed by the Secretary of State. The consequences may not be apparent to the uninitiated, but they are important. At Ascension, whatever money is wanted to be spent is procured by the commanding

value, or to fulfil these conditions. It is therefore necessary to draw attention to the fact that the Imperial roads round the Cape and round Cape Horn cross each other at a point on the Equator about 25° W. If a comparatively small circle with that centre be described on a mercantile chart, it will be found to include the path of nearly all vessels passing along those roads. It therefore follows that the defence of the sea area so included is of the greatest importance to Australasia and Eastern and Pacific possessions, and that it would be useless to distribute force for the protection elsewhere of the commerce of those places unless we can command that small area. But we cannot maintain a patrol at these Imperial

---

naval officer, asking the Admiral to sanction it in the name of the guardship stationed there—say the old ' Flora '; and whether the sum be 20l. or 20,000l., is practically the same; the expenses of Ascension are never brought before Parliament, and the only thing a curious inquirer can find out is that a guardship at Ascension is always the most expensive vessel in the Navy. Now St. Helena, being placed under the Colonial Office, has to provide for its local expenditure by local taxation, and should anything beyond this be required, it must be introduced into some parliamentary vote and be subjected to parliamentary questioning. Yet there is as good reason for the one island being supported by Imperial funds as the other, and many distinguished officers, both naval and military, have advocated this view. In his latest Governor's report, Vice-Admiral Patey, who is a good authority on professional subjects, says that ' the situation of St. Helena in mid-ocean renders it a most important position for Imperial purposes as a coaling station and depôt for vessels of war.' Moreover, if we were engaged in hostilities, the sinking of a ship in the Suez Canal might close that passage, and then St. Helena would be hardly less valuable than Malta or Gibraltar. ' Two or three steamers stationed here,' says Admiral Patey, ' would intercept the whole returning trade from the East.'"—*St. Helena Guardian*, May 7th, 1874.

cross roads without bases of operation from which that force can draw supplies; we have no choice, therefore, but to adapt Sierra Leone and Ascension to the purpose of fulfilling this Imperial requirement. It is further essentially necessary for the safety of Australia, and the East, that these points should not fall into other hands,* and if we do not adopt measures for their defence, there is nothing to prevent such a contingency.

Now, though the Imperial strategic points I have named are numerous, I think it will be found difficult, even on close inspection, to reduce the number without risk to the safety of the Imperial lines. It must be remembered that a point near a line of communication, if not secured to our own use by means of defence, is placed more or less at the disposal of our enemy. The position we abandon, because we have others in its neighbourhood, may be of vast strategic importance to the power having none. The immense and Imperial importance of the great majority of strategic points named cannot, I think, be much doubted, and therefore for purposes of illustrating general principles requires no further remark. We have seen

---

* **South Africa.**—" A colony is not now removed from danger of attack by remoteness, and the vessels which England in case of war should furnish to defend her colonies, must plainly be, during war time, independent to a large degree of home support."—*The Natal Mercury*, May 23rd, 1874.

"The defence of the Empire may possibly become a popular cry when it is too late to save many of its most valuable outlying portions."—*Port Elizabeth Telegraph*, May 23rd, 1874.

that military garrisons are required to prevent their capture by assault.* Where are they to come from? What provision has the Empire made for the safety of positions which command her roads?

It is our boast that we are at last secured from invasion, because we have 100,000 regular troops at home. But when we are threatened with invasion, we are in imminent peril of investment. As the regular army is the only military force we can move, it clearly follows that, if 100,000 or

* **West Indies.**—"India is quite able to hold her own against any foreign attack; she has nothing to fear whilst she remains firm in her allegiance to the sovereignty of England. With regard to the Australian colonies and Southern Africa, they are strong by natural position and their remoteness, and every day their strength is growing, and with it their capability of self-defence. Coming to the Western Continent, what has Canada to fear, except from an invasion by the United States, a bordering country, whose inhabitants speak the same language, enjoy the same free government, belong to the same race, and are equally interested with themselves to live at peace, to carry on trade and agriculture, and to develop the resources of the immense territories covered by forest and prairie within the limits of each, reaching to the Pacific Ocean? As for the West Indies, they must go with the maritime supremacy; while it remains in the hands of England, no foreign power would venture to disturb them, or think it worth their while to fit out an expedition for their conquest."—*The West Indian*, April 7th, 1874.

Australia.—"The geographical position, conditions, and resources of Canada and other colonies referred to by Captain Colomb are so dissimilar to those of Australasia that we need not descant on them here. Neither do we think it necessary to follow him in his surmises and prognostics regarding the possible victory of the Americans in the West Indies, and how far such a conquest would affect the safety of our North American dominions. These problematical difficulties but retard the proper study and drift of the question. They lend no weight to the argument they are made to sustain, and the argument itself is a weak one."—*Sydney Morning Herald*, June 8th, 1874.

any large proportion of that number of regular troops are necessary to guard against invasion, no force is available for garrisons of places on which the safety of our communications depends. We should have to choose, at such a time, between risking invasion or courting investment, partial or complete. When this argument is used it is generally met by the assertion that we have, or shall have, a powerful fleet, and therefore shall command the sea. Now the "command of the sea" is a vague term, conveying no precise meaning to the mind. It is, from its vagueness, most valuable to mystify constituencies, or to confuse the conception of our true military requirements, both in times of "panic" and intervening periods of "parsimony." By war ministers it is used alternately to lull the awakened consciousness of military weakness, or as an argument for the reduction of military force. To most people it means something purely naval. To some it conveys the idea of covering the seas with numerous fleets; to others, the possession of a few ships more powerful than those of our neighbours. Few realzie that the command of the sea can only be maintained by a scientific combination of three things—strategy, purely military force, and purely naval power. The command of the sea is nothing more nor less than the command of the Imperial roads, the securing of the first lines of colonial defences.

It is important to bear in mind that the more war fleets rely on machinery and artificial motive power, the more necessary are fixed bases of operation to their action, and the greater must be the resources of those bases. Hence it is that, as the science of naval warfare advances, the necessity for developing these resources at the great strategic points, and for efficiently protecting them, will probably increase.*

But "an ounce of fact is worth a pound of theory"; and while others dwell on the political results of the exploits of the 'Sumter' and 'Alabama,' it is desirable not to lose sight of the lesson in Imperial Defence the cruise of these vessels teaches. Captain Semmes, writing on board the 'Sumter,' in the West Indies, remarks: "The enemy has done us the honour to send in pursuit of us the 'Powhattan,' the 'Niagara,' the 'Iroquois,' the 'Keystone,' and the 'San Jacinto.'"

* Australia.—"This is indisputably and suggestively true. All along our lines of communication the more assailable positions must be strengthened, and their natural resources developed and protected for England's advantage. The importance of coaling stations, for instance, cannot be overlooked. These are indispensable necessities in these days of steam warfare. England possesses almost a monopoly of this material force, and she can judiciously expend it. Strongly-fortified islands might be made depôts for coal, in case our cruisers' supply became short. Many spots of our Empire might be selected: Fiji has been mentioned as one. The value of these islands has been enhanced by the establishment of the San Francisco mail service, and their suitability as a place of call is now beyond dispute. They form, too, a middle point of defence between Australia and Vancouver's Island, and would be either a great strength or weakness to us in the event of a war, say with America. Let them be made a stronghold as well as a coal depôt."—*Sydney Morning Herald*, June 8th, 1874.

Not one of these vessels ever caught her, and if we read on we shall see the reason. "The Mona Passage being the regular track of U.S. commerce, it was looked upon as almost a certainty that at least one cruiser would be stationed for its protection." The supposed certainty, however, was a delusion. Months afterwards we find Captain Semmes exclaiming, "Where can all the enemy's cruisers be, that the important passages we have lately passed through are all left unguarded?" And then he sarcastically adds, "They are off, I suppose, in chase of the 'Alabama.'" Again, he said: "The sea has its highways and byways, as well as the land. . . . If Mr. Welles had stationed a heavier and faster ship—and he had a number of both heavier and faster ships—at the crossing of the thirtieth parallel, another at or near the equator, a little to the eastward of Fernando de Noronha, and a third off Bahia, he must have driven me off, or greatly crippled me in my movements. A few ships in the other chief highways, and his commerce would have been pretty well protected. But the old gentleman does not seem to have thought of stationing a ship anywhere." [*]

It is impossible that anyone carefully studying the cruise of the 'Sumter' and 'Alabama,' can avoid the conclusion that we have had to pay 3,000,000*l.*, not so much for letting the 'Alabama' escape, but as compensation to the United States

[*] 'My Adventures Afloat,' by Admiral Semmes.

for damage directly resulting from the vague notion the head of their naval department had respecting the "command of the sea," and his utter incapacity as a sea-strategist. All the naval force of the United States was powerless to arrest a single ship in her progress, simply because it was applied without reference to general principles which guide the distribution of force for the protection of communications.

It is important to observe that there is no proportion between the force used in the interruption of sea communications, as compared with the amount of force required to secure them. To cripple the action of a single steamer we find it acknowledged, by one who ought to know best, that several cruisers would be required at certain points. A regular attack upon sea communications, therefore, involves the employment of an enormous force in their defence; and as the stations and positions are necessarily fixed, so must bases of operation be at hand to supply the wants of that defending force.

There is, however, another lesson we may learn from the cruise of the 'Alabama,' which, if we profit by, is well worth 3,000,000*l*. to our Empire. It is the value of coal to offensive and defensive operations at sea. We find considerations regarding the consumption and supply of coal constantly regulating and limiting the action of the 'Sumter' and 'Alabama.' While we congratulate ourselves that "even the stores of coal needed for marine locomotion are principally ours," we must remember that they are only ours so long as we protect them from destruction by bombardment or from capture by assault.* It is therefore of paramount importance that our coal depôts along the Imperial lines should be efficiently and thoroughly defended; that they should not be selected at haphazard, or situated at places in the possession of any foreign power when it can possibly be avoided.

The closing scene of the career of the 'Alabama' is, however, yet more instructive to those who have the defence of the Empire at heart. True, she was sunk near to our own coast, almost in English waters, by the guns of the 'Kearsage,' but if we would know what it was that forced her within the range of those guns we must carry our thoughts far away to the Indian Ocean. In the far east we find Captain Semmes writing as follows: "My ship will have to go into dock to have much of her copper replaced, now nearly destroyed by constant cruising, and to have her

* India.—"We must have our coaling stations well protected. What is the use of our depôts for coals if any of the enemy's fleet have simply to proceed and destroy them? In the West Indies, as Captain Colomb states, 'the great coaling station, St. Thomas, is not in our possession.' Some people are inclined to argue that we have the command of the seas. Command with what? With steamers, with the coaling depôts not secured, with no arsenals well protected from bombardment, where they might obtain munitions of war, with no docks secure from an enemy's fleet."—*The Englishman*, Calcutta, April 24th, 1874.

boilers overhauled and repaired, and this can only be done in Europe." And so to Europe the 'Alabama' came. Defective and without adequate means of repair, she was no longer able to efficiently fulfil her mission, nor quite free to choose the fields of her action, so, dragging her damaged boilers and dilapidated hull down the Indian Ocean, round the Cape and up the broad Atlantic,* she sought refuge and repair in a French port. The rest of her story is soon told. Denied the means necessary to restore her to her original efficiency as a ship of war, and with defective ammunition, she was compelled to engage an antagonist, whose challenge she was from her condition neither fit to accept nor able to avoid. In seventy minutes she was sunk. For want of means of repair in the Eastern hemisphere she lies beneath the waters of the English Channel, silently warning us to profit by the lessons she has taught.

There is one other popular view respecting the command of the sea to which it is necessary to refer. It is that the command of the sea can be secured by the blockade of our enemy's coast. The experiences of the American war throw some light upon this argument. In the *Singapore*

* "On May 2 we recrossed the Equator into the northern hemisphere . . . and ran up to our old tollgate, where, as the reader will recollect, we halted on our outward passage and *viséd* the passports of so many travellers. The poor old 'Alabama' was not now what she had been then. She was like the wearied foxhound, limping back after a long chase, footsore and longing for quiet and repose."—*Vide* 'My Adventures Afloat,' by Admiral Semmes.

Times of December 9th, 1863, we read: "From our shipping list it will be seen that there are no fewer than seventeen American merchantmen at present in our harbours. Their gross tonnage may be roughly set down at 12,000 tons. Some of them have been lying here now upwards of three months; and all this at a time when there is no dulness in the freight market, but, on the contrary, an active demand for tonnage to all parts of the world. It is indeed to us a home picture—the only one we trust to have for many years to come —of the wide-spread evils of war in modern days. But it is a picture quite unique in its nature, for the nation to which these seventeen fine ships belong has a navy perhaps second only to Great Britain, and the enemy with which she has to cope is but a schism from herself, possessed of no port that is not blockaded, and owning not more than five or six vessels on the high seas. The tactics with which the Federals have to combat are without precedent, and the means to enable them successfully to do so have not yet been devised."

It is as well to remark, that at the time this was written the naval force of the Federals consisted of about 700 ships and some 40,000 men! Yet it was not equal to preventing the interruption of American commerce in distant seas, although it maintained a strict blockade of the enemy's ports. Now Singapore was a neutral port, and therefore afforded protection to the Federal vessels; but where are the available ports likely to be neutral, along our lines, to afford protection to our commercial fleets under similar circumstances? The natural rendezvous of commercial fleets are in our possession, and could only afford protection in proportion to their means of defence.*

By securing bases of operation for our war fleets, we also provide safe refuge for our traders at places where it is most required. If ever we are in real danger of invasion, we shall be actually engaged in a naval war; we shall not have the excuse that the tactics we have then to combat "are without precedent"; but we may bitterly regret that the means "to enable us successfully to do so have not been devised," not from lack of power, but from want of will.

While it is essential to guard the strategic

* **Hong Kong.**—" What we say is, that every place of such commercial importance as Hong Kong should be properly fortified, and so fortified that, in the absence of a defending fleet, the enemy would find it no easy job to obtain a good position in front of the city for placing his guns.

"What we have said as regards Hong Kong, would probably apply in a greater or less degree to all ports of call between here and Suez; and although we can hardly be expected to take as much interest in the protection of other places as in this, yet we doubt not their inhabitants would gladly join with ours in making such a representation to Parliament as will convince them of the facts that we are in no way protected, and that for the interests of the British Isles it is necessary that we should be. As to the question of cost, we must defer that to another time, when we hope to be able to point out the way in which it should be divided amongst the colonists and those living at home."— *Overland China Mail*, May 9th, 1874.

Note.—No article relative to the distribution of cost, here referred to, has reached me.—J. C. R. C.

points from capture by military force, it is equally necessary to secure their resources from destruction by bombardment from the sea; and in many instances military force would be—from natural circumstances and situation—powerless to prevent such a contingency. The destruction of certain coal depôts might be accomplished in a few hours by a single ship with very few guns; and heavy requisitions, on pain of instant bombardment, might be hastily levied on a fleet of merchantmen in harbour by " an intelligent maritime Uhlan " in the shape of an insignificant crusier, even in the presence of military force. This danger can in several instances only be met by port defence vessels, and torpedoes. A very small local force, if trained and provided with these weapons, would meet the requirement. But where are the weapons? Where is the force ? It will be too late to await the outbreak of war to provide the weapons and to train the force, for an attack on our coal depôts at the strategic points will not be the last, but the first act in the drama of future war. The means for their destruction are always at the disposal of any maritime power, but the measures for their adequate defence take much time to develop. A single cruiser bringing her guns to bear on one of our coal depôts, would in a few hours paralyze the action of our fleet for months.

It is not possible here to enter more fully into details respecting the defence of the Imperial roads, which is the first, and can be made the strongest line, of colonial defences. In no way can our colonies and possessions be so efficiently protected as by a firm command of their communications, for, with the exception of Canada and India, they would thus be exempted from the possibility of attack, and unless Canada and India are to be cut off from succour and support, their communications must be held, come what may.

The lines of colonial defences may be thus summarized :—

1. The defence of their communications, which involves fortifying the Imperial strategic points, and the existence of a purely naval and a purely military force ; the one equal to the task of keeping open the roads between the points, the other sufficient to secure those points from capture in the necessary absence of the fleet.*

* India.—We have only to look to the case of the ' Alabama,' sunk in English waters, because she had no place to refit, no dock to which she might proceed 'to be overhauled, and have her boilers repaired.' So, without sufficient ammunition, and in her imperfect state, she was sunk in seventy minutes. Have we a large naval arsenal in the Eastern seas? Have we port defence vessels? Are all our harbours protected by torpedoes? And, if they were, have we a body of men instructed in their use? It would appear as if we laboured under the opinion, in case of war, that our enemies would never think of bombarding our ports, of interfering with our commerce, of destroying our supplies of coals, or of attacking any of our possessions. We have withdrawn our troops from the colonies, and we have said to them, ' Protect yourselves,' and we have given them no arms and no guns, so that they might follow the advice given. We have five millions of surplus at home, a large portion of which is derived from our customers ; and we are oblivious of the fact that, if they ceased to exist our revenue might possibly decrease."—*The Englishman*, Calcutta, April 24th, 1874.

2. The interior line of sea-defence, which must provide against the destruction, by bombardment from the sea, of naval resources at the strategic points in cases where that object cannot be secured by land batteries and military force. It also includes similar provision for the protection of colonial mercantile ports to prevent their commercial reduction by enormous requisitions.

3. The defence of the soil of all colonies and places not necessary to the Empire as military and strategic positions.

Having thus briefly viewed the nature of our requirements, it is desirable to draw some practical conclusions as to how they can best be met.

The communications of the Empire being the common property of all its component parts, each portion, according to the use it makes of them, has a direct interest in their defence, and should contribute to that object.*

---

* **Australia.**—" The Royal Colonial Institute is no doubt a little in advance of the times, but perhaps there is no harm in that, for speculative opinions expressed within the bosom of such an association are sure to be wholesomely modified by the intense repugnance which the practical British-Colonial mind has to the consideration of questions involving the fortification of strategic points, and other matters of high Imperial consideration. Great as is the support which we now receive from our intimate and attached relationship to the mother country, it would be vain to deny that in the event of war, the interests of British commerce and of international comity might be subserved in a higher and more Imperial sense by the absolute independence of the federated Canadian or Australian colonies than they could be by the fortification of strategic points as recommended by Captain Colomb. We have said ' in the event of war,' but a war between Great Britain and a combination of great maritime powers is not a contingency which we can at present contemplate. Meanwhile, let us avoid that, and taking counsel

The forces intended for the defence of the communications must be Imperial, and not colonial. They must be prepared to act at any point on the Imperial lines where they may happen to be required. Naval colonial volunteer forces which may be created under the Naval Defence Act of 1865 are only of value, and that to a very limited extent, to meet the necessities of the second or interior line of colonial defence.

The forces necessary for the defence of the Imperial communications should be under the control of one directing head. As military force is necessary to the support of naval power, and as in our case military force is in its turn dependent upon naval power, the distribution of the one must have reference to that of the other. If, therefore, the military force is under the control of one department, and the naval force under that of another, the defence of our communications is, to use a homely phrase, "between two stools."

from the source of all good counsel, let us keep our powder dry, and work on towards union and strength among ourselves."—*Brisbane Courier*, June 11th, 1874.

South Africa.—" We need not say that the plan suggested is based on the presumption that the colonies, being interested in keeping open the Imperial roads, would contribute towards the cost; that it contemplates a system of mutual co-operation between Great Britain and her colonies; that it presupposes federation, or the consolidation of provinces or small colonies into territories or dominions; or that it leads almost inevitably to that great confederacy of the whole Empire which some may deem chimerical, but which we firmly believe to be the only real solution of the anomalous relations now existing between the colonies and the mother country."—*The Times of Natal*, June 24th, 1874.

In vain might our "Admiralty" despatch fleets to distant seas, if the bases of their operation are not secured by the "War Office"; equally valueless would be the distribution of military force for the protection of those places by the War Office, if the Admiralty do not keep the communications between them open. Unless there be a war minister responsible for, and controlling the general principles which should govern the action of each department, nothing but confusion can result when the Imperial communications are in danger.

If the colonies are really in earnest in matters relating to their defence, it is time they should combine to force on the attention of the Imperial Parliament the neglected state of the Imperial roads, and the necessity for devising adequate means for their security. They must, however, be prepared to bear their fair share of the burden.*

If the mind of the mother country is morbid, and, from dwelling continually on the terrors of invasion, has lost the power of comprehending the

---

* New Zealand.—"Imperial and local interests manifestly run concurrent here, as they do in reality throughout. But the difficulty is to impress that fact upon the colonists. Theoretically they might agree with Captain Colomb upon the importance of maintaining the Imperial lines of communication; but if he asked them to accept the logical conclusion, and help to pay for the defence of those lines, they would draw back. They have become so accustomed to shirk their national duties, that it will take a long while to get them out of the selfish groove which they find so pleasant, but which is rapidly denuding them of patriotism, and making them a set of mere money-hunters. A great calamity might possibly awaken in them a nobler spirit."—*Wanganui Chronicle*, June 5th, 1874.

consequences of investment, it is time her young and vigorous offspring should awaken her to a true sense of her position.

A Royal Commission to inquire into the defence of the Imperial communications, if properly constituted on an Imperial basis, would lead to most important results. It may be taken as a certainty that such a Commission would recommend the permanent strengthening of the great strategic points, which it would be in a position accurately to define. It might possibly determine the just limits of Imperial and colonial responsibilities in the question of defence.*

---

* **Canada.**—"We quite agree with the gallant lecturer, that a federation of the Empire is a necessity—that a federal fleet and a federal army are requirements of the day, and that the defence of Great Britain, as well as of its most insignificant dependency, is incomplete without it. We are also certain that the colonies are prepared to pay their share of the cost, as well as to bear their share of the burthens; as far as Canada is concerned, no difficulty would be found in applying any portion of her army to Imperial purposes if necessity required, nor would she be wholly defenceless as far as naval power is concerned; one of her people (Sir Hugh Allan) controls the largest and finest line of ocean steamships possessed by any company in the world—vessels that would realize the gallant captain's idea of efficient ocean cruisers in the amplest sense of the term."—*Volunteer Review*, Canada, January 27th, 1874.

Natal.—"Let us hasten, then, to claim a part in this great work; first throwing aside the leading strings which cramp our action; then multiplying our strength by a close union with the southern continent, of which we form a part; lastly, by urging in the Council of a great federation such a policy as the paper before us indicates. The cry will soon be raised by other colonies; will, ere long, swell into a universal chorus; let us, though one of the smallest and weakest, not be the last of the great British family to claim our share in this noble and patriotic scheme."—*The Times of Natal*, June 24th, 1874.

West Indies.—"England must follow the example of ancient Rome,

With the creation of Imperial fortresses commanding the Imperial roads would grow up a feeling of common security. They would be links in the chain which binds together the military forces of our Empire; stepping-stones by which those forces can cross to, afford mutual assistance and support.

Such a Commission, and such measures, might

and give to all her colonies and foreign possessions the right of citizenship and the name of British subjects, and of being considered integral parts of the British Empire. It is due to her greatness and to the maintenance of her position amongst the foremost nations of the world. If she is content to limit her dominions to the British Islands, and desires to cast off her colonies and to leave them to work out their own destinies, she must withdraw from the first rank and give place to the United States, Russia, France, and Germany, and see herself, at no long distance of time, reduced to a level with her own colonies in Canada and Australia. But we cannot believe that this is the view taken by British statesmen, Liberal or Conservative, of the question, or which would be sanctioned by the British Parliament."—*The West Indian*, April 7th, 1874.

Malta.—" Captain Colomb's paper appears to us to contain suggestions of the highest importance ; and a Royal Commission, as proposed by him, would tend to enlighten both the Government and the public concerning the defence of the Imperial communications to be established on an Imperial basis. Inquiries of such magnitude and importance can only be made in times of profound peace like the present, which are also most suitable for the taking of such defensive measures as shall efficiently protect from a combined attack all the parts of the Empire to which England owes so large a share of her wealth and commercial prosperity."—*Public Opinion*, Malta, April 1st, 1874.

The Cape.—" Captain Colomb recommends the issue of a Royal Commission to inquire into the defence of the Imperial communications, and we cordially endorse his recommendation. This seaport, for instance, is at present defenceless, and yet, by a small expenditure, in the event of a war between England and another naval power, it might be protected from the depredations of some new ' Alabama.' A few Armstrong guns, with the needful ammunition and a few torpedoes from the Imperial stores, with the Naval Brigade resuscitated, would impart a sense of security to the community it has not felt since the commencement of the Crimean War. A federation of the war forces of the

prepare the way for a federation of the war forces of the Empire, which is essential to its safety. It would be easier in a given time to collect forces from all parts of the Empire at a given point now, than it was to concentrate the military forces in the United Kingdom on any particular place on the coast line sixty years ago. It is singular that when science has done, and is doing, so

Empire is indeed essential to its safety."—*Port Elizabeth Telegraph*, May 23rd, 1874.

Australia.—"Captain Colomb urges the colonies, if they are really in earnest in matters relating to their defence, to combine to force upon the attention of the Imperial Parliament the neglected state of the Imperial roads, and the necessity for devising adequate means for their security; but he warns us that we must be prepared to bear our fair share of the burden. And this is where a great difficulty would arise, for in time of peace—when alone such a scheme could be carried out—it is to be feared many a colonial legislature would fail to see the necessity for voting the requisite money, and the Imperial Government would be powerless to enforce payment."—*Queensland Times*, June 4th, 1874.

"A Royal Commission for such a purpose might, no doubt, attract attention to the subject, and prepare the way for a consideration of that much larger subject, which includes the confederation of the British Empire. The Duke of Manchester tells us that in this matter we of the colonies should claim this as our right. That is to say, he tells us we have a right to be an integral part of an Empire of which at present we are only dependencies. We should assert a right not only to contribute to the maintenance of these strategic points, but to guide and control the policy which maintains them. But, as his Grace says, 'the House of Commons is so apathetic'; and we fear we may add the colonies are also. They are growing, it is true, in wealth and strength, but as yet they are scarcely educated into a perception of the full benefits of these Imperial privileges, and of the Imperial responsibilities which await them. In the meantime, we here in Australia have scarcely yet entered on the threshold of the inquiry. We have not yet taken the still more needful and preliminary step of providing, after the example of Canada, for a Federal Government, competent to deal with questions involving such serious international questions."—*The Brisbane Courier*, June 11th, 1874.

much to increase our power of concentration, Imperial policy should be undoing her work by persisting in the creation of local forces which it is impossible to move, and all this at a time when concentration is the great principle of attack, and the power of concentration is the great principle of defence. Though by nature and by science we possess all the physical means necessary for the concentration of military forces, we have neglected to turn them to account, and further, by limiting the action of military forces to the particular portions of the Empire where they are raised, we wilfully destroy the necessary power of resisting concentrated attack by a combination of Imperial resources, which is in these days the true source of strength.

It is only in maintaining the second line of colonial defences that local forces are of real value, but it is the duty of the Empire to see that they are provided with the means and weapons to enable them to act. For the first and third lines they are of no avail, so long as the necessary power of concentration at the weakest point is absent. It is military necessity, and not constitutional law, which determines where the greatest power of resistance is to be applied.

While we acknowledge and applaud the principle, that it is every man's duty to defend his home, it is to be regretted that our ideas of its practical application are lamentably indistinct.

The mother country has put her own construction on the word "home," in applying the principle of calling into existence military forces which can only be used to put up her shop shutters and to bar her doors. She calls on her children to adopt her definition of its meaning and to follow her example, and some have done so. But who among the armies thus organized, for what she is pleased to call "home defence," can determine the exact distance from a man's home at which the obligation ends? Who can draw the magic circle which is to include the territorial area of his duty to die for his country? Home is something more than an abstract idea having reference only to locality; its foundations are laid in common interests, sympathy, and affection. A "silver streak of sea" cannot divide these interests, nor can miles of ocean sever the strong ties of affection and of sympathy. Hence it is that, from whatever quarter of the Empire a cry for help comes—wherever the British flag waves over Englishmen struggling on their own ground for all they hold dear—it is there our home is in danger, there is the rallying-point of forces created for its defence.

While we boast of armed hosts here and in the colonies, whose proud motto is "home defence," they must "survey the Empire" to "behold our home." *

<small>* **Canada.**—"Our immediate interest in all this arises from the position we occupy to Great Britain—politically and strategically—a point that has been lost sight of by the statesmen of the Manchester School;</small>

but one which affects the interests of the Empire in no ordinary degree, nevertheless, and deeply concerns ourselves.

"In the event of a great European war, it will be absolutely necessary for Great Britain to set her house in order. There can be no new trials. Our position geographically and strategically is such that we can to a very great extent compel our neighbours to look to their own concerns, and to make it their direct interest to take the part of Great Britain in the quarrel; thus keeping open a vital source of supply—food—for her people.

"If this is to be done effectually, British statesmen must be up and about their business. An adjustment of the *naval* and military relations of the Empire must precede a federation of its dependencies, and the defensive movements must no longer be confined to the *hedgerows* of England. With her own power consolidated, and the United States as an ally, Great Britain may bid defiance to the world in arms."
—*The Volunteer Review*, Ottawa, February 2nd, 1875.

CHAPTER IV.

IMPERIAL AND COLONIAL RESPONSIBILITIES IN WAR.*

IN 1873 I had the honour to address this Institute on the subject of "Colonial Defence." As the remarks I am about to offer as a basis for discussion here and in the colonies are but a continuation of that paper, I must briefly refer to general views and principles it formulated.† It is necessary to do so for the reason that they were honoured by great consideration at the hands of the colonial Press. One of the chief objects of this Institute is to bring to a focus colonial opinions, so that national shortsightedness at home may have the assistance of Imperial spectacles;‡ and

---

* Read before the Royal Colonial Institute, May 1877.

† **Australia.**—" It may seem ungracious to become impatient with people whose only fault is an over-anxiety for our own safety; and yet the patronage of such fussy busybodies is very irksome. Captain Colomb believes that he has a mission to awaken the home Government and the colonial moiety of the Empire to a sense of the dangers which threaten them from the inadequacy of the means of defence in the Pacific."—*Melbourne Leader*, Victoria, July 28th, 1877.

‡ **Australia.**—" Considerations of this kind all tend to show that colonial federation is indispensable to our future security, as anything like common action is almost impossible without it. We are aware that there is, in Victoria, a political party which is in favour of neutralizing that colony. But what naval power at war with England would consent to such a neutrality? A successful raid upon Melbourne would be worth

therefore as one of its Fellows, I shall best fulfil my duty by submitting to special notice such views and arguments as are adverse to those put forth in that paper, omitting for the present all reference to still more numerous expressions of cordial approval.

In a matter of such vital importance as Imperial Defence,* the main question at issue is this: How to secure with economy, yet truly and efficiently Imperial safety? When any solution of that great problem is suggested—and I grieve to say no one besides myself has ever yet considered the question as one great whole—more attention should be paid to arguments calmly and deliberately urged against its adoption, than to any outburst of sentiment, however general, which advocates its off-hand acceptance. War sweeps away all "castles in the air," all false sentiment, and leaves nothing standing but bare, naked facts. It crumbles to dust false ideas and false hopes, and consolidates the power of one Empire by scattering to the winds the fanciful delusions of another. Therefore in considering questions relating to defence, it is most important not to trust sentiment too far, but to weigh calmly and carefully practical arguments.

from 5,000,000*l.* to 10,000,000*l.* to the war-chest of the nation making it; and Victoria, in order to neutralize, must first denationalize herself."—*Queenslander*, August 4th, 1877.

* New Zealand.—" The chief peril of war to England is, not so much the conquest of its colonies, as driving them to the conviction that their safety lies in secession, that is, in becoming neutrals."—*The Colonist*, Nelson, August 21st, 1877.

The paper to which I refer was a sketch of our Imperial position, the dangers to which it is exposed, and the strategical operations necessary for its safety. It may thus be briefly epitomized:—

(1) It brought to view the fallacy that colonial defence can be considered as an abstract question, or that national defence can be limited in its meaning to the defence of the United Kingdom.

(2) It pointed out that the principle of "home" or "local," or "domestic defence," if indiscriminately applied, as it has been by the wholesale creation of forces which cannot be moved from the soils on which they are raised, must produce Imperial weakness, not Imperial strength.

(3) That the United Kingdom is merely the "grand base" of the Empire, that for this reason it must be rendered secure, not only from capture but also from having its communications cut near home. Were the latter contingency to happen it would be helpless as regards itself, while it would cease to be of any value to the rest of the Empire with which it could not then communicate.

(4) That even supposing the United Kingdom secured both against invasion, and the interruption of its water roads near home, there yet remained to be effectually guarded against as pressing and as serious a contingency, viz. partial investment by an enemy operating against one or more of its communications, with the other portions of that Empire of which it is but the heart and citadel.

For example: an opposing naval force operating with St. Helena as a base, at the crossings of the South Atlantic, would cut the whole of the Imperial communications round both Capes; and were the Suez Canal to be blocked at the same time, the whole Empire, except Canada and the West Indies, would be locked out from its grand base, and the United Kingdom would be partially invested.

(5) That we can only secure the Imperial water roads, first, by a firm, strong grasp at all times of the points which command them; second, by fleets adequate to the requirements of keeping free and open the lines between the points.

(6) That those fleets would be paralyzed in their action if the points between which they are to operate are not held by military forces sufficient to render the protection of the sea-going fleets unnecessary; or, if there are not in addition at these points, stores of coal and means of repair adequate to the requirements of the fleets of which they are the base.

The reasons for these conclusions will be found stated shortly in that paper, and at greater length in other papers and works I have put forward during the last eleven years. They have never been disputed, and though they were most unpopular eleven years ago, because we could think of nothing at home but our own personal safety, they are now happily attracting attention. The "génie" of the British Empire* is rising out of the "pot" of the United Kingdom in which it was too long confined. May this "spirit" never be "asked to go back to show where it came from," and let us hope the time is approaching when Englishmen will cease to talk of their "country," and at all times and under all circumstances act as citizens of a Great United Empire.

On the conclusions referred to were rested the following propositions:—

1. That as the Imperial strategic points had been and are utterly neglected, the colonies should combine to force on the attention of Parliament and Governments the necessity of providing means for their security and of increasing their naval resources.

2. That a commission properly constituted on an Imperial basis, should be appointed to inquire into this matter, and that such a commission might determine the just limits between Imperial and colonial responsibilities in the question of defence;

* Australia.—" The unity of the British Empire is now more than ever a prominent theme of discussion in England. Nor can we be surprised at this. How best to encourage and promote the closest relationship between the mother-country and the colonies may verily be considered one of the questions which most vitally concern the welfare of Britain, as well as the immediate future of her outlying possessions. The doctrinaires who glibly prated about the advantages of a policy of separation, and whose whims and speculations were for a season countenanced by a section of the British Parliament, have been silenced, so that we hear nothing that is worth heeding about the advantages of retiring from India, abandoning Gibraltar, or leaving Canada and Australia to go their own ways."—*South Australian Advertiser,* August 14th, 1877.

and that thus might be prepared the way for a federation of the war forces of the Empire for purposes of defence.

3. That an absolute and pressing necessity exists for the erection of a great Imperial dockyard at the other side of the world, which would relieve the pressure on home dockyards and fulfil duties they cannot in war perform, and in peace offer commercial advantages of construction and repairs to ships of the mercantile marine.

4. That some change appears necessary in the administration of our war forces, because as the protection of the Imperial roads is partly naval and partly military, there is no one controlling power over both; the Admiralty may scatter fleets in one direction, the War Office tie up military forces in another, but there is no power to combine the two, and without such combination each branch of our war power of defence would be helpless.

5. *That as the communications of the Empire are the common property of all its compound parts, each portion, according to the use it makes of them, has a direct interest in their defence and should contribute to that object.**

---

* **West Indies.**—"Imperial and colonial interests are identical and it is the duty of both the mother-country and her colonies to take a fair proportion—according to wealth, population, and the nature of the duty required—of the labour and sacrifice which the preservation of the common heritage demands. It may be difficult to prescribe or define the area of duty which should be allotted to each component of the Imperial aggregate, but we are convinced that the true loyal policy

Lastly. That forces created for the defence of "home" must "survey the Empire," in order to behold that which they are to defend.

Now an exceedingly able writer in the *Sydney Morning Herald*,* took great exception to some of these views. He says: "We want—we require no standing army here. If England does her duty, this colony at least will do hers. Increased and stronger harbours and coast defences, and a gradual filling up of the ranks will go far to protect all we hold dear. Besides, in these days of rapid communication, additional troops can be landed on any shore: there is always sufficient warning of impending danger to enable the Imperial Government to send assistance to the places most likely to need it . . . . It is argued that fragmentary self-reliant forces are of no use, for to be of any value they must be fitted to move from one attacked point to another. Now this strikes at the root of what may be called our system of domestic defence. New South Wales, for instance, should not, cannot indeed, be asked to pour her defenders into Ceylon, or the West Indies, nor would she expect to be similarly assisted. The only movable troops are those of the Imperial army. They ought to be shifted from one threatened or assailed place to another, as the occasion demands. The self-reliant

is to consider the interests of one as the interest of all."—*Jamaica Colonial Standard*, July 16th, 1877.
* 6th and 15th June, 1874.

isolated armies of the 'fragments' of the Empire will do yeoman's service on their own ground, and that is all that may be expected of them. That is the reason of their being, and that is the object of the movement which has met with such laudable success. . . But we need not follow Captain Colomb further, unless it be to record another disagreement between us. He believes that any expense incurred in repairing 'the state of the Imperial roads,' ought to be shared by the colonies. We think not. We impose no burdens on the mother-country for the maintenance of our safety ashore; and so long as we are integral portions of the Empire, we believe it is her duty to keep the roads in repair. Hr honour and supremacy are dear to us all; but they concern herself first and principally. Our share of the obligations we willingly do, and to the statesmen of Great Britain we look for the rest. . . . . Self-defence and self-reliance must be watchwords, and each colony will do its duty if it provides a force sufficient to protect its own territory." *

I submit these passages to special notice, as they are directly opposed not only to the views stated at length in my former paper, but will not be found in accord with my further remarks to-night. They form a candid, fair, and straightforward expression

---

* **Australia.**—"As our readers know, that is practically the system which Sir William Jervis has been carrying out. He is visiting each colony and arranging for each its own entirely separate system of defence."—*Sydney Morning Herald*, August 3rd, 1877.

of that colonial opinion which is adverse to the adoption of any Imperial scheme of defence, as will be presently seen. Those few brief but weighty words, extracted from two very lengthy and very able articles, very favourable in other respects, are deserving of most serious attention. They cover the whole ground of possible objections to acknowledging that any Imperial responsibility rests on any fragment of the Empire outside its own boundary, save and except that portion called the United Kingdom. The truth is, that while every portion of the Empire now happily recognizes fully and absolutely the necessity for defending it as one great whole, opinion as to responsibility, if not much divided, is at all events left utterly undefined. Before, however, proceeding further I will give two passages from that remarkable paper, "Fallacies of Federation," which must be taken in conjunction with what I have already quoted. "It must be borne in mind," says Mr. Forster, "that so long as any colonies are British colonies the British Government is bound to protect them, and would protect them in case of war . . . . and Great Britain is also bound to bear, and could not avoid bearing, the chief cost of such war." Taking this last passage in connection with the general statements of the address from which it is extracted,[*] I conclude the chief cost means the whole cost, less only the expense of such local and purely defensive

[*] *Vide* 'Journal Royal Colonial Institute,' vol. viii., 1876–77.

works and forces colonies choose to create or maintain. Any colony may or may not provide means of defence. The British Government cannot, in an Imperial sense, compel it to do so, nor exercise control over the constitution or distribution of such local forces or means of defence,—if created,—beyond colonial limits. The fact of a colony not adopting of its own free discretion means of defence adequate to its requirements, or to the best of its ability, simply increases the responsibility of the British Government. The responsibility, therefore, of the Government at home in the matter of defence becomes greater in exact proportion as a sense of responsibility on the part of the colony diminishes. The less a colony does, the more must the United Kingdom do. Now this is not a matter merely between an apathetic colony and the mother-country, but it affects every portion of the Empire, because the extra war power necessary to put forward for the safety of that colony is just so much deducted from the force available for the protection of other Imperial fragments.

There can be no doubt that "so long as colonies are British colonies, the British Government is bound to protect them" to the very best of its ability; and there can be no doubt also that "self-defence and self-reliance must be our watchwords." The point is, however, are these watchwords to be used in an Imperial sense, binding all Englishmen under an Imperial standard which they combine to defend, or is each Englishman to have a little flag of his own, and hoist it where he sees fit, and try to defend it or not, as he feels inclined?*

The question to be first settled is this: What is protection? What is defence? It is really only chasing shadows to devise schemes for the protection of our colonies; it is only a dreamer's fancy to arm for defence and to emblazon flags with "Self-reliance," if we are not clear what it is we have to protect, what it is we have to defend. Are we going to protect the unity of the Empire, or merely to prepare to save what we can out of a possible wreck? Are the strong to defend themselves, and let the weak perish? Are Englishmen behind "increased and stronger harbours and coast defences" at Sydney to regard with complacency the capture of Fiji; to hear without dismay the seizure of King George's Sound; or that the foe had established a base of operations at New Guinea, or in still more suitable positions on some of the neighbouring islands? I feel certain the able writer of the article would in the presence of such contingencies be inclined to think that the honour, wealth, and supremacy of magnificent Sydney was concerned "first and principally," and that so long

* **Hong Kong.**—"The colonies have duties to the mother-country as well as claims upon her, and it is only by recognizing them properly that a spirit of unity will be kept up between them. It is a good sign that Englishmen are gradually growing proud of the British Empire rather than of the British Isles, and to feel that it means something far mightier than the seat of government in Europe."—*The Daily Press,* Hong Kong, July 23rd, 1877.

as Sydney could spare a single man or had a single shilling available to help to prevent such a catastrophe she would not have done her duty did she not spend that shilling and dispatch that man. I rather fancy that the writer now so strongly in favour of rooting all military power of defence to the particular soil on which it is raised, would then fling away his pen and carry a sword across the sea for the safety and honour of that Sydney he so dearly loves.

I do not ask for "standing armies in the colonies." I only submitted that the several parts of the Empire should come to a common understanding as to the defence of the Imperial strategic points, such, for example, as Fiji and King George's Sound, and in proportion to the extent to which their honour and wealth is concerned in the security and efficiency of these positions, so should they contribute in common with the mother-country to their maintenance and safety as Imperial strongholds.*

If the colonies think it is wholly and solely the duty of the people resident in the United Kingdom to provide for the safe keeping of these Imperial

---

* **Australia.**—" Yet imagine the hue-and-cry which would be raised by the demagogues in the Victorian Assembly if any treasurer should have the temerity to propose placing a sum of money to assist in placing either or all of those points in a state of defence! ' What!' they would exclaim, ' send money out of the colony for the benefit of our neighbours? Spend our taxes in providing employment for "foreigners," whom it is the object of our fiscal system to injure and impoverish? Never, never, never.' "—*Queenslander*, August 4th, 1878.

keys, they should insist that they do it; they should not allow measures vital to their own safety to be so completely neglected. There is no use concealing the fact that the British Government, labouring under the pressure of home constituencies possessing all the power, cannot be reasonably expected to move far in such a matter except supported by counter-pressure from without. It is idle to forget that if cavalry and field artillery be deducted from the strength of the regular army—our only movable force—the number remaining would not provide the strategic points of the Empire with garrisons, much less furnish expeditionary forces, which the colonies imagine we can at any moment "throw on any shore." The Imperial roads cannot be kept open unless such places are secured independently of the protection of sea-going fleets, and therefore if the mother-country and her colonies do not come to some common and really Imperial understanding as to how these places are to be provided with sufficient garrisons, adequate defences, and naval resources, a great war will find our fleets helplessly watching their bases, while home and colonial merchant ships are being chased over the ocean like hares by *Alabama* greyhounds. The injury to commerce, the paralysis of trade thus caused will be the "chief cost" of such a war. It will fall on the mother-country and her colonies, not regulated by our own theory of responsibilities in matters of defence or warlike preparation, but practically *pro rata* on each portion of the Empire, according to its commerce and trade, the strategical advantages its territory offers for seizure or requisition, and its relative geographical position to the quarter from which the opposing war power is launched.

Whatever therefore may be a true or false theory of responsibility in matters of our defence, war against us will not be waged on any theory whatever; it will visibly press upon, and be most felt by the interests most exposed to attack, and leave us to settle our "*Alabama* claims" and our damages and accounts as best we can among ourselves. It is hard to say therefore, beforehand, on what portion of the Empire the "chief cost" will in the end fall. If Fiji or King George's Sound were captured, Australasia would feel it most; were Singapore or Hong Kong taken, each part of the Empire would suffer in proportion to its India and China trade; and so on. If our squadrons are tied to these places because they are not defended nor have adequate garrisons in war, the water districts of which they are the centres would be left without efficient protection, and similar results follow.*

---

* **New Zealand.**—" Let us hope that, in due time, there will be an Australian and New Zealand militia, trained in the arts of modern warfare, and not unmindful of the solidity of the whole Empire. In this hope, we think there can be no doubt that the colonists of Australia and New Zealand will heartily join."—*Hawke's Bay Herald*, July 31st, 1877.

"If," says the writer, "England does her duty, this colony (New South Wales) at least will do hers .... There is always sufficient warning to enable the Imperial Government to send assistance to the places most likely to need it." Clearly, then, he considers it the duty of the people living in the United Kingdom to send military force to every place "likely to need it." If this be a correct view, it is as well the whole Empire should know England has not prepared to do so. While she now, as of yore, expects "every man to do his duty," Englishmen in the colonies rightly expect she will do hers. But the very essence of the whole question lies not in the sentimental expression of a readiness either on the part of England or the colonies to do their duty, but to distinctly comprehend practically what are the duties to be done. When Mr. Forster says, "the mother-country is bound to protect her colonies," let it be asked in what way? Is her responsibility unlimited? And are the colonies not bound to help? Does it extend not only to guarding all the trade lines of each particular colony, no matter in what direction they lie, but also all English homes and interests scattered over territories in the aggregate sixty times her size? Are colonies neither to furnish men nor money according to their means to help the people of the United Kingdom to do so? In that case the signal of Trafalgar must be reversed so far as the colonies are concerned. It must stand thus: England does not expect every man to do his duty, but every man expects England to do hers!

I am sure Mr. Forster differently construes the word "protect," and is very far indeed from thinking that the colonies have no duties and no responsibilities in this matter of defence, or that Englishmen whose lot is cast in the colonies instead of at home may absolve themselves from all obligations lying beyond their own shores, while, on the other hand, those who live in England cannot by any means do so. In the latter case, an Englishman can vary his responsibility by simply changing his residence from one part of the Empire to another.* At home he can be taxed to protect water communications, the safety of which is a common necessity to all; but in the colonies he can escape the obligation. This is surely a very

---

* The political aspects of the question must be left to others to discuss. It would be out of place to consider difficulties presented by internal Imperial policy in a paper which deals with the external pressure of war. If that policy weakens our power of resistance, we must take the consequences; we cannot make the war operations of our enemy subservient to our particular ideas of government. The reader who wishes to follow up the subject in its political aspects, will find ample matter for close study and grave thought in the 'Proceedings' of the Institute, and in 'Imperial Federation of Great Britain and her Colonies,' by F. Young. It is also but right to draw special attention here to a passage in Mr. Forster's paper previously referred to: "The British Government and Parliament have no right to inflict this revolution [Federation] upon any colony or group of colonies, unless with the *full consent* of the colonists concerned, or *unless it can be shown that such a course is absolutely necessary for Imperial interests, for the interests of the Empire generally, in short, for the interests of us all.*" [The italics are mine.—J. C. R. C.]

strong argument in favour of a general exodus from England to the colonies on the eve of war. There is too much reason to fear that rather than grapple with a great difficulty which deeply concerns us all, we Englishmen at home and abroad try to hide it from our sight. We are but too apt to believe there is a wide difference between Imperial and Colonial responsibility in war: we entirely forget that no home or Colonial Legislature, no power and no man, has ever yet even attempted to draw that line which is supposed to divide distinctly the one from the other.* I would submit that there is no such line; that there can be none. The problem of Imperial security cannot be solved by disintegrating that which is common to all; it is a burden resting proportionably on every fragment of the Empire, and distinctions are not those of responsibility, but simply of practical ability.†

---

* **Bermuda.**—" When the question of federating the provinces of British North America, as they now exist, under the Dominion of Canada, was being discussed, the Hon. Joseph Howe, of Nova Scotia, proposed the broad question, which underlies Captain Colomb's entire thesis, of the federation of the Empire. And the day is fast approaching when a practical consideration of the matter will be forced on us by the sequence of events, as regards the commercial relations between England and her colonies."—*Bermuda Royal Gazette*, June 3rd, 1879.

West Indies.—" It is the common duty of England and her numerous colonies to share the cost and labour of defence, but the great question that wants solution is how to distribute this responsibility and duty."—*Jamaica Colonial Standard*, July 18th, 1877.

† **Australia.**—"*But while we have no control over any diplomacy, no word to say about the Eastern question, or any other question, no power to determine*

The weak must bear the burden according to their strength. The problem is one, not of division, but of adjustment. The misfortune is, that Imperial policy has been directed, not towards adjusting the burden, but has really thrown it down, leaving the United Kingdom and the colonies to cut off bits here and there according to selfish, mistaken instincts of self-preservation, and the result is that much of it remains repudiated by both. No one can say to whom the heavy remainder belongs, whether to the mother-country or to the colonies. We will not pick it up, because we have taken all the "home defence" out of it we require; the colonies will not touch it, because they have cut off as much "domestic defence" as they think they want. To understand what that remainder is, it is necessary to examine closely our existing arrangements for the defence of our Empire.

"Each colony," says the article, "will do its duty if it provides a force sufficient to protect its own territory . . . . our share of responsibility we willingly do, and to the statesmen of Great

---

whether we shall go to war or remain at peace, there is no political reason for asking us to defray the cost of a war in which we have no voice, and perhaps no interest. There is nothing in this view of the case that is selfish; it is simply a corollary from the admitted doctrine that taxation and representation go together."—' Sydney Morning Herald,' *August 3rd*, 1877.

Britain we leave the rest." This quotation furnishes a very brief but most distinct idea of the prevailing notion existing in men's minds of the allocation of responsibilities in war. Let us examine its practical value, and take New South Wales as an example. It has a population of some 600,000 souls, scattered over an area of some 323,000 square miles, and an enormous assailable coast line, offering numerous safe places for landing troops. No very large proportion of rural population so scattered can be made really effective for military service. In that splendid essay * by Mr. Reid it is stated that 27 per cent. of the whole population of the Colony is to be found in the metropolitan district of Sydney. These two facts taken together show that on that district rests the main responsibility of protecting the whole colony. The forces for the protection of its territory consisted in 1875 of a naval brigade mustering 329, and military forces 4646, all told, about one-third of which is made up by cadet corps furnished by colleges and public schools; 3000 therefore about represents the available military force. Our ablest Engineer officers are already considering on the spot works of defence. Doubtless they will point out a pregnant expression used by the greatest engineer England ever produced: † " My fear would be of establishing works at very considerable

---

* 'An Essay on New South Wales.' By G. H. Reid.
† The late Field-Marshal Sir John Burgoyne, R.E.

expense, and afterwards being forced to abandon them for want of troops." If New South Wales is to be left when attacked entirely to its own military resources, any extensive works might have to be abandoned. The fortifications of Paris did not save France, nor can forts at Sydney save New South Wales in the absence of sufficient garrisons. Without such forts at Sydney and Newcastle the action of a movable army and a movable fleet would be completely crippled; but the forts without this army and this fleet, and without sufficient military force to defend them, would be monuments of extravagant shortsightedness. A power in possession of Sydney or Newcastle, and also King George's Sound, could hold in an iron grasp the whole continent of Australia. In the safe custody of those positions is the whole continent "first and principally concerned." Each colony in that continent has an equal and direct interest in the safety of such places. If, therefore, colonies are not responsible beyond their own boundaries, if they are under no obligation to share the military expenditure necessary to secure places because they are beyond their political limits, and if these forces cannot be moved out of the colony in which they are raised, it all comes to this—the population of Sydney must be responsible for the safety of one-half the continent, and whatever Englishmen happen to reside in the vicinity of King George's Sound must be held responsible for the other.* But their responsibility does not end here, for if these points are lost the trade and commerce for a huge area around them are lost also. " Trade follows the flag," and the flag that waves triumphant over Sydney and King George's Sound will determine the nationality of the trade on the great districts of ocean of which they are the "strategic points." This is not a thing merely affecting the interests of those Englishmen who happen to reside at those particular places. It "first and chiefly" concerns Australasia, and is of vital importance to the whole British Empire. Thus does this principle of "home or local defence," indiscriminately applied, place an Imperial burden on a few individuals, not because they are most capable of bearing it, not because they are alone interested, but simply because they have the misfortune to live at places of Imperial strategic importance. Such points are most liable to attack because they offer enormous advantages as naval and military positions. When attack is resolved upon it will be delivered with such imperial or national impetus as may be deemed sufficient to offer reasonable prospects of success. The means of attack will be furnished by the available resources of a great nation; the nature and amount of force employed for the pur-

* **Australia.**—" We know that our volunteers are not worth much, but such as they are, we should decidedly object to their being taken away to garrison King George's Sound."—*Melbourne Leader*, July 28th, 1877.

pose will be determined by the necessities of the particular operation — by nothing else. These necessities will be estimated by our means and method of resistance. Concentrated energy of Imperial or national power may be brought to bear on the point selected for attack. Now, suppose either Vancouver's, King George's Sound, Fiji, Newcastle, Sydney, or any other point, be so selected. If our power of military resistance at such places be regulated not with reference to the Imperial importance of the position, nor to the nature and extent of defensive work to be done, nor yet by the possible force of attack, but simply by a rule-of-thumb system of arming and drilling whatever Englishmen happen to live there, the result of contact is not a matter for speculation or for hope—it is a miserable certainty. The simple truth is that power of attack means power of concentration; and if in defence power of concentration be absent, weakness is opposed to strength, and a very natural result follows " the survival of the strongest."

Again: there can be no doubt whatever that if a colony has no commerce, no trade, and no interests beyond its own boundaries, it will have done its duty if it provides forces sufficient to protect its own territory.* But the glory of New

* **New Zealand.**—" In the literal sense, it cannot be said that any colony answers this description, though, if the underlying principle is considered, it may very well be contended that it includes most of the Australasian settlements. Their trade is almost entirely confined to

South Wales is her external trade. "According to population her external trade average," Mr. Reid tells us, "is more than double that of the United Kingdom." Those who maintain that there is a distinction between Imperial and colonial responsibility in war, and that the responsibility of a colony ends on its shores, must answer this question : Why should the people of the United Kingdom pay and find the force necessary, and be responsible for the protection of the "external trade" of New South Wales, when the proportion of individual interest is as one to two? Again : but one-third of the total exports and imports of New South Wales comes to and goes from the United Kingdom. Why should the Englishmen at home be responsible for the protection of the other two-thirds which neither comes to nor goes from them, while those "first and chiefly concerned" look on from behind the "stronger harbour defences" of Sydney with all their resources and war-power carefully locked up?

These are questions which cannot be shirked by believers in "home defence indiscriminately applied," nor passed over by those who differ from

the purchase of articles not grown or manufactured within them, and the sale of gold, wool, or other raw material, that would find a market just as readily on the Continent of Europe or in the United States as in England. There are really no ties of interest to one country rather than the other, and this narrows the question of defence to their own territory."—*The Colonist*, August 21st, 1877.

my humble opinion that there is no such thing as a distinction between Imperial and colonial responsibility, and that in war all must share, according to their several ability, the Imperial burden of defence. But, putting aside all this, surely it is a fallacy to assume that any colony can " protect its own territory." Is each fragment —nay, is any fragment of our Empire, single-handed and alone, a match for any power which can possibly attack it? Could each particular colony in Australia defy the power of the United States? Is it at all certain that New South Wales, the greatest of them, is a match for Russian power on the Pacific? Mare Island, the United States naval arsenal, is but 6460 miles, and Vladivostock, the Russian base, but 5000 miles, from Sydney. The Russians moved without steam power military forces, stores, and guns backwards and forwards in 1854, over a sea-line nearly 900 miles long, in the North Pacific, in complete defiance of the combined naval forces of France and England. It is not wise to rely entirely on the power of fleets to prevent the despatch of expeditionary forces from either Vladivostock or Mare Island. There is no physical impossibility to prevent either power working from these bases to transport a complete corps of 5000, without any great effort, to the shores of Australia. In war the only matter to be considered by them is the reasonable prospect of success. This prospect of success can only be estimated by our preparations for defence.* In inverse proportion to our preparations for resistance will be the arguments in favour of attack. The less we have the power of concentration, the more possible is success to those against us. King George's Sound and Sydney command the Australian Continent; but under existing arrangements either power, in contemplating operations which would, if successful, carry the whole Continent, has not to consider the force of resistance furnished by the whole Continent, but simply to calculate the military strength of Western Australia as regards King George's Sound, and of New South Wales as regards Sydney or Newcastle. Is it to be supposed that either of the two colonies named could protect their own particular territories from the assault of 5000 disciplined, probably picked men, ably commanded, furnished with accurate maps, possessing full and detailed information, and backed by the resources of a great nation? It would not be the inhabitants of Mare Island; it would not be the residents of Vladivostock appearing at Sydney, Melbourne, Newcastle, Perth, Adelaide, Hobart Town, or King George's Sound, to measure swords with the populations of each place. It would be the concentrated pressure of a great nation scientifically brought to bear on

* **Australia.**—"The theatre of a future war would not, as before, be the Mediterranean and the Black Sea alone; the Pacific would offer a more promising field to an enemy."—*Perth Inquirer*, Aug. 11th, 1877.

the lungs of Australia, in order to leave her prostrate or to mar her life. The advantage to be gained by such an operation is an Imperial or national advantage, while under our " home defence " arrangements the military resistance to be overcome would be but fragmentary, or, in other words, colonial. The principle of local defence, which prevents the concentration and combination of the whole war power of Australia, is one of the strongest possible inducements for attacking favourable positions there, in order to reduce each colony in succession. Are we to assume that because Australian colonies, each separately, are physically unable to furnish local forces sufficient to protect their own particular territories, they are each to be considered as having failed in their duty?* If we are alone responsible for their safety, have we no right to insist upon a combination or federation of the war power of the great Continent? Are they at liberty to increase our responsibility, and our difficulty in defending them by objecting to combine their forces?† Is

* **Australia.**—King George's Sound is in this position: an enemy's fleet can occupy it to intercept the steamers carrying the mails and carrying the gold, and can also sally forth to capture the ships arriving from England. Although there are no coal mines in the neighbourhood, there is always sufficient coal in hand to replenish the bunkers of a hostile fleet. Western Australia must be treated as a Crown colony, and the defence of its principal harbour (King George's Sound), if it is thought worth defending, must rest with the Imperial authorities, until the colony grows strong enough first to share the burden and then to take it all.—*Sydney Morning Herald,* August 4th, 1877.

† " No doubt, if Australia were federated for general intercolonial

the burden of Imperial responsibility to be shuffled off by the mother-country and the colonies by a hap-hazard apportioning of our respective duties, without regard to our respective resources, and without reference to any consideration, but a pitiable desire to be rid of it? These are all questions which must be answered by all those who see distinctions between Imperial and colonial responsibilities, and who therefore argue against the federation of war forces for purposes of defence.

Again, all colonies are not practically taking the same view of preparations for defence. Some are doing much towards providing military means to resist attack, others are doing little or nothing. In a general war, are the people of the United Kingdom to "help those who helped themselves," or are their efforts to be chiefly directed to protecting those who by their own neglect have rendered themselves more tempting objects of

purposes, or even simply for defence purposes, the care of all the necessary strategic points would fall on the common fund. But separated as we are at present in our governments, we could not, if we would, combine for the defence of King George's Sound, even if we feel strongly that we had a common interest in doing so: for we have no official machinery through which we could act, and our intercolonial jealousies would prevent that decisive action which is essential to success in all military operations. There is no alternative, therefore, but to leave a post of that kind to be dealt with at the discretion of the Imperial Government, and the only possible way in which the colonies could help at present would be by a *pro rata* contribution towards the cost of the Imperial defence of the place; just on the same principle as we make a contribution at present to the civil establishment at Cape York."
—*Ibid.*

attack? Without some binding federal arrangement as to the distribution, organization, and maintenance of war power, the colony that buried its talent in peace may in war reap the solid advantages of assistance from us at the expense of others who meanwhile have made ten. But, more than this, are the residents in the United Kingdom to be left to give or to withhold assistance at will, and be free from any binding federal obligations? Or are they to be expected to have real Imperial strength without the power to draw from the whole Empire, in proportion to the resources of its several parts, 'real Imperial power? If there be distinctions of responsibility in war, these questions must be answered. They must not be left to be settled when war comes, to chance and "English spirit." Sentiment without system means in these days defeat and disaster. To take a practical illustration. Canada, with a population of some three and a half millions, furnishes an example to the English race. Her commercial progress in peace does not blind her to the necessity of being prepared for war. She takes a calm view of her position, and arranges to meet possible events. She taxes her financial resources, and calls on all her sons to do their duty, and willingly do they respond. Possibly some day or other, the eyes of the world may be fixed on North America, watching a life and death struggle for the honour of the English name. In such a case are other fragments of the Empire to despatch correspondents to give interesting accounts of the proceedings and—nothing else. The naval power of the United States, drawn from 10,000 miles of Atlantic coast, would, if we do not prevent it, be concentrated on the St. Lawrence. Considering that an Englishman in Canada bears a far heavier military burden than an Englishman in the United Kingdom, surely, in common justice, we would be bound to sacrifice our whole naval power rather than permit her being invested by blockade. This involves our sending, besides a naval force superior to hers, a strong war garrison to Halifax, and a movable and purely military force for strategical coast distribution, and for counter attack. But let us turn to the South; are we then to leave Bermuda without force, and abandon to their fate the English West Indies? Our only movable military force, which is also the reserve for India, is but 100,000. This force would be at once absorbed by requirements in the West Atlantic. We may be in no danger of invasion at home, and sorely pressed for troops abroad, but meantime we shall have a military force of 300,000 men in the United Kingdom, which the principle of "home defence" has made it impossible for us to move.* It is illegal to send them where they

* **Australia.**—" It may be maintained that if a defensive force is liable to be removed, it ceases to be a defensive force. This is precisely the point on which the colonies and the Home Government disagreed at

are required; therefore they must remain where they are not wanted, and look on at Englishmen being slaughtered, with the calm consciousness that, thousands of miles away from the fight, they are striking examples of the principle of self-reliance, and fulfilling Imperial responsibilities in war.

But supposing this estimate of probable requirements to be exaggerated, and that some force, naval and military, could be spared for service in other parts of the globe, is it quite certain that, in the absence of binding federal obligations, the people of the United Kingdom who really have control would readily part with force? The Colonial Office would be pulling one way, the Admiralty in another, and the War Office in a third, while public attention at home would be fixed upon the fact that its trade and commerce is brought to a focus in and about the Channel. The principle of "self-defence and self-reliance" is as applicable to naval power as to military force, and if we are true to our principle, colonies need not be surprised at its results. Our greatest trade centres are near home, and where our greatest danger appears to be, there, in obedience to the dictates of this principle, have we the right to concentrate more power than may be

---

the time when the Imperial troops were withdrawn. The colonies were willing enough to pay for the maintenance of these troops in times of peace, provided they were not withdrawn when war broke out."—*Melbourne Leader*, July 28th, 1877.

really wanted if we see fit. Public opinion at home, with the Government in its hands, free and unfettered by any binding federal obligation, might in a panic possibly insist upon keeping the residuum of our movable forces at home. There would be some justice in the assertion that as the United Kingdom alone pays and finds the only movable forces, other parts of the Empire have no real ground of complaint if these forces are distributed without regard to their special requirements. Many arguments might at such a time be produced in favour of retaining forces at home. It would then be remembered how in 1778 Paul Jones in the *Ranger* defied our fleets, harassed our home trade, landed at Whitehaven, seized the forts, spiked the guns, set fire to the shipping, and even carried off Lord Selkirk's plate from his seat on St. Mary's Isle. Economists would point out that in the war between 1775 and 1783 eighty-two men-of-war were taken from us, besides 118 of our war vessels being destroyed or lost, and that this was the expensive result of England's fighting all over the world. In the popular excitement produced by a threatened commerce, in the chaos of our war administrative systems, and in the absence of binding federal obligations as regards defence, it is not impossible the necessity of upholding the integrity of the Empire at any cost and at any risk might disappear before constitutional clamour for the adoption of a policy of "self-reliant isolation."

Point might be given to such views by reference to the fact that long ago the colonies had been told to arm themselves and to be self-reliant, and that as they were satisfied with it in peace they must take the consequences of its results now that war had come.* They might be told "we could not swop horses when crossing the stream." Such pictures may be considered too highly coloured, but let it not be forgotten that without any such sharp incentive as actual danger for centralizing and tying up our only movable forces, that is the practical policy we are steadily and noiselessly pursuing now. We have a national (?) mobilization scheme which has taken years to elaborate, and in that scheme there is not even an indirect allusion to any place lying beyond the chalk cliffs of Dover. More exclusive attention year by year is being directed to the construction of such types of vessels as are useless for service on distant seas; while millions have been and are being spent on extending home dockyards which are but little use for the efficient maintenance of fleets at the other side of the world.

Let us now glance at the possible condition of the Pacific Ocean. Even granting we blocked the

* **West Indies.**—"The interests of the mother country and her colonies are so bound up together and so thoroughly identical, that whenever this great fact is ignored, and negligence or selfishness is allowed to obscure and impede the operation of a true patriotic policy, the injury is felt not only by the offended member but by the central heart and, to a greater or less extent, throughout the whole organization."—*Jamaica Colonial Standard,* July 16th, 1878.

Atlantic ports of the United States, the safety of Australia, New Zealand, Fiji, and Hong Kong will then be in proportion to the force and vigour of Canada's resistance or power of counter attack. If it be sufficient to absorb the purely military power of the States any concentrated effort on any of the points named would be hardly possible; but if not, several thousand men might be poured into, say Fiji, before a single detachment of troops from England or India could reach it. For Pacific territories to assume " there is always sufficient warning of impending danger to enable the Imperial Government to send assistance to the places likely to need it" is to forget geography. Vladivostock is 8000 miles, and Mare Island some 7000 miles nearer Sydney than Plymouth. The great Pacific railway across the States effectually settles the question of time; it has shortened by months the possible concentration of American military force on any point in the Pacific. On the other hand, within the last twenty-three years, complete water communication for 2200 miles from the interior to the Pacific has been acquired by Russia, and within the last four years her naval base on her Pacific coast has come down some 800 miles nearer Hong Kong and Australia. Before the Crimean war her military forces were barred out from the sea by some 200,000 square miles of intervening territory then belonging to China. That war rendered it necessary for her to burst the barriers. While we pressed her in on the Baltic and Black Sea, she bulged out on the Pacific. Her military forces are now spread over seaboards and territories formerly Chinese, and their headquarters is now 3000 miles nearer Australia than in the year 1854. She has one advanced military post within fifteen days' steam of Vancouver, and another within eight days' steam of Hong Kong. The Russian naval force in the Pacific is practically independent of European arsenals, and that of America entirely independent of Atlantic dockyards, while our Pacific fleets have to rely for support on Portsmouth and Plymouth, and can only receive stores and reinforcements round the Cape or through the Suez Canal, and our military force is caged at the other side of the world.

In view of such developments in the North Pacific, Australia is vitally concerned in the honour and supremacy of British naval power in that region. It is necessary to her security that it should be well guarded. Our fleets must keep that sea; they cannot do so without coal. Nature has provided it, and British instinct of a former age, ignorant of the value or even of the existence of this all-powerful element, secured to us the place of its abode—British Columbia. Our power of keeping the sea in the North Pacific rests entirely and exclusively on our ability to secure British Columbia against all attack, and in guarding this North Pacific gem, set as it is with black diamonds, we shall be establishing a post naturally capable of Imperial strength, about as near Australia as Mare Island. It would be an outwork against that steady advance of Russia which sooner or later will shift the real Eastern question from the Mediterranean to the Pacific. It would also "hold a pistol to the head" of San Francisco. Being 1000 miles nearer Sydney than Panama, Australia could regard the cutting of the Isthmus of Panama without any very great apprehension of its strategical consequences. I may remark that the cutting of that canal will considerably modify the view of the able writer already quoted, and a time may come when a certain island in the West Indies may be in reality an Australian Gibraltar. But how has this huge Empire, with all its wealth and intelligence, acted with regard to British Columbia? It has left it shut out from succour, it has left it to sink or swim, because to connect it by railway with the Atlantic would cost some 10,000,000*l.* and might not pay for some time. Canada must be self-reliant and make it if she wants it, and leave it alone if she does not want it.

Now, the United Kingdom has within the last five years thought it worth while to pay.7,000,000*l.* on account of water communications; 4,000,000*l.* has gone into the Suez Canal, through which but one twenty-eighth of our total commerce passes; and 3,000,000*l.* has gone, no one knows where, as a fee for Captain Semmes' lessons in sea strategy, by which we have not profited. But for a work of immense value in peace and in war, vital to our Imperial life in half the world, we cannot afford to pay 10,000,000*l*. Thus the Empire is ready to cast down its North Pacific pearl to be trodden down by "swineherds," whose name is—shoddy. We shall only have ourselves to blame if it is picked up and placed in the Imperial crown of Russia, or added as one more star in the flag of the United States. As we have seen, a day may come when Australia will watch with anxiety the operations of the Canadian army, so her fate may hang on a naval action fought at or near Vancouver's Island. The hauling down of the Union Jack in British Columbia would be the ominous warning to all our Pacific territories that the hour had come when the ferocious national war strength of our enemy could "strike at the roots" of our innocent little systems of "domestic defence." Not only is Australia deeply concerned in the Canadian Pacific Railway, but it is a matter of vast importance to us at home. As I have for years persistently pointed out on every possible occasion,*

---

* "It may be perhaps excusable to repeat the concluding passage of lectures on 'The Distribution of our War Forces,' delivered at a time when the ghost of invasion frightened the word Empire out of England: 'As regards the United Kingdom—the citadel of the Empire—let it never be forgotten that we have two dangers to guard against—direct assault and investment, partial or complete. Though these islands may bristle with bayonets, though, at the very name of invasion, millions of riflemen may be ready to line the hedgerows, let us not shut our eyes to the fact that our supplies might be cut off, that we could

these Islands must not only be guarded against invasion, they must be also secured against investment. As our population increases, so can the successful chances of invasion be made to diminish, but so also do the dangers resulting from investment become more possible and more serious. Increase of population in the United Kingdom means more mouths to feed, more numerous claimants for national out-door relief. We are a great people, but we must have food. We at present buy in the cheapest open market, but it never seems to have struck us that there can be such a thing as an Imperial co-operative store, and that the site of the butcher's and baker's department lies between the Red River and the Rocky Mountains, and that all we want is a road to it. We forget, also, that in making this road we should also be making a short cut to the infinite supply departments of Australia, Tasmania, and New Zealand. But we have up to this been so busy preparing for invasion that we have not had time to think of these things. In the event of war with America the mouth of the Mississippi will be closed, the American "Golden Gate" of the Pacific will be shut, and the other lines of our food supply will be objective points of attack by swarms of cruisers.

be, in short, starved out. Therefore must our war forces be distributed in such a manner as will best secure the Imperial base of operations, and ensure safety and freedom of our Imperial communications."—*Journal Royal United Service Institution*, 1869.

No hostile squadrons may hover close round our shores, yet we might be in imminent danger of investment, and might possibly feel the stress of hunger.* We keep Bermuda and Halifax as Imperial fortresses to provide for the contingencies of war with the States, and yet take no thought how, in that event, we are to feed our people at home. If such a war takes place before the British Pacific Railway is made, we may bitterly regret we spurned Nature's gifts profusely spread at the foot of the Rocky Mountains. With empty stomachs we shall have no "spirit left in us" to retaliate for the loss of British Columbia, and Australia may then call in vain for help. With that railway and consequent cultivation and development of this "fertile region," the forces necessary to keep open Canada's communications would at the same time guard our food supply, and also protect the Atlantic side of the short cut to Australia. By thus making it possible for one force to perform a triple duty, we should free two-thirds of our available naval strength, and thus all other parts of the Empire not so directly concerned in this line of defence would proportionably benefit. Surely, then, as a defensive work this railway is an Imperial question, and not simply a

* **New Zealand.**—" Neither Danube nor Rhine would be of equal interest with the scanty meals of thousands of families. England might fight for the Balance of Power without much sympathy from those doomed in consequence to suffer hunger."—*The Colonist*, August 21st, 1877.

colonial concern. This is a part of that heavy remainder of the Imperial burden of defence we pass by. Telegraphic communication is another. While Russia has connected her naval bases in the Pacific with a continuous wire from St. Petersburg some 6000 miles long, we cannot afford to lay 2000 miles of wire to connect our great coaling port of the North Pacific with London. Russia can put her Pacific armies and fleets in motion three minutes after the order is given from St. Petersburg. We can only send messages through United States' officials, who are not responsible to us if they never reach their destination. This is our application of the principle of "self-reliance"! It is but the logical result of the system of "fragmentary self-defence." British Columbia can have neither armies nor fleets to move, and therefore telegraphic communication would be perhaps superfluous. We have some ships scattered over the whole ocean. There are no works of defence raised by Imperial hands at British Columbia, no forts for the protection of our coal, nothing but *prestige*, sixty-nine militia,* and a few constabulary guards it from attack,† while a powerful Russian fleet is already concentrated in this quarter of the

---

* See Official Report of No. 11 Military District of Canada, 1876.

† **Canada.**—"Anything more thoroughly defenceless than our position it would be difficult to imagine; it would almost seem from its helplessness that it was thus placed to invite attack and afford an enemy the opportunity of being easily supplied with naval stores." — *The British Colonist*, 1877.

Pacific waiting events, and its officers openly talk of taking Vancouver's Island. If that point is left to be protected by our fleet, our naval force must be concentrated there. The Russian squadron has then a clear road to Australia. Supposing we try to blockade that squadron now at San Francisco, we may get into difficulties as to neutrality bounds with the States; it may, besides, slip through our fingers, as it did in 1855 in Castries Bay. In the latter case our fleet may go in hot haste to Vancouver's, to find the coals burned and the mining works destroyed, and to learn the enemy with full bunkers has left for Australia, whither our fleet cannot follow because it cannot get coal. Thus it is that the principle of "self-defence indiscriminately applied" to British Columbia vitally concerns Australia, and leaves it open to attack.

For some reasons or other it is assumed that in the matter of the defence of the Empire, the protection of the sea and the defence of the land are two separate and distinct questions: that colonial responsibility is bounded by sea, and what is called Imperial responsibility is bounded by land; that colonies have none beyond their shores, and that with some few exceptions, Imperial duties of defence are strictly and entirely confined to the sea. It is on this assumption we have based our preparations for defence; it is this theory which has produced huge military forces, "fixed as the monument on Fish Street Hill," and which cannot move across the sea or pass from one colony to another, even though nothing separated them but a political boundary. We have at home 400,000 troops. Three-fourths cannot be moved across the sea, and nearly one-half (the volunteers) cannot even be moved to Ireland. "The self-reliant armies of the fragments of the Empire will do yeomen's service on their own ground, and that is all that may be expected of them." It is, therefore, very evident that both the United Kingdom and the colonies at present seem to believe there is neither reciprocity nor commonality of responsibility so far as land defence is concerned. The result is that when we are threatened with invasion at home we can look for no military help from abroad, and when the colonies are threatened abroad they can get no military aid from home.* We may be in no danger of invasion, and with a military force, at the very least, of 300,000 at home, we are to let British Columbia, or the West Indies, or all our colonies go rather than give military help. The Cape may let St. Helena, the Falkland Islands, and the Mauritius go rather than move a man. Queensland must not mind Fiji

---

* **Australia.**—" And in the meantime the British Empire, vulnerable at so many points, is, for defensive purposes, a heterogeneous mass of incoherent atoms."—*Queenslander*, August 4th, 1877.

" We wish we could impugn the accuracy of these statements, but we fear it is impossible; and we cannot do better than submit them to careful consideration as constituting arguments which appear to us to be perfectly unanswerable, in favour of Australian federation, as one great step towards Imperial federation and Imperial safety."—*Ibid.*

being captured, nor New Zealand Tasmania being taken; nor must New South Wales mind Victoria being overrun, nor Victoria stir a military finger though the enemy be encamped at Adelaide; and South Australia must look on while a hostile force occupies King George's Sound. We impose no burden (say the colonies) on the mother-country for the maintenance of our safety ashore, therefore they must defend themselves. We impose no burden on them, therefore we must defend ourselves; and so the system of territorial defence may thus be shortly summed up—every place for itself and the Empire for none!

But weak colonies, having neither population nor resources sufficient to make even a faint show of military preparation, sometimes get a little doubtful as to the efficacy of this newfangled doctrine of military disintegration. Mr. Forster comforts them with the assurance that the British Government at home "is bound to protect them in war." But faith in the logic of these words is somewhat disturbed by the logic of these facts—that the British Government at home ties up its military forces and omits mentioning such places altogether in its great mobilization scheme. This creates alarm, and then we quiet them by pointing to our fleet. We give all our colonies to understand that the fleet will, without any army, make up for every deficiency in the matter of land defence here, there, and everywhere, all over the

world, and they believe it. But they must remember we ourselves do not believe it. We have created a military immovable force 300,000 strong because our Channel fleet cannot be relied on to protect an assailable coast line from the Humber to Penzance, only 750 miles in length. How, then, are ships scattered over a world of water to be relied on single-handed to protect territories with thousands of miles of undefended shores?*
Further, our fleets cannot keep the sea without the support of an army distributed strategically over the face of the globe to secure their bases. Our existing arrangements lock up our military forces, and provide no garrisons for the Imperial strategic points. Our fleets cannot move far away, therefore, from those places when expeditionary forces are on the sea. They cannot leave their coals to be taken or burned, nor risk the capture of their stores and means of repair. The truth is, the principle which ties up our military forces in immovable detachments also will bind, with strong chains of necessity, our fleets to

---

* **Australia.**—" In the case of South Australia the direct advantage of having British men-of-war in these waters is trifling indeed. One of Her Majesty's ships engaged in cruising in the Pacific, enters our ports occasionally : but the visits, like those of celestial beings, are short and far between. Beyond this, what reliance can we place upon these vessels, and what security have we that in the hour of danger they will be at hand to assist us ? Simply none at all. Adelaide might be sacked and burned while H.M.S. ' Nymphe ' was at Fiji, and the latter might be occupied by an enemy while the 'Nymphe' was in Australia."
—*Adelaide Observer*, 1877.

their own depôts. In adopting this principle of fragmentary defence, which deprives us of the power of concentrating naval power or military force, we are forgetting our past history, and doing our best to deprive all British territory and all British sea lines of intercommunication of efficient naval protection in war. Our military weakness is not so much a want of force as a self-imposed inability to apply it where it is wanted. This system was not devised by the British Government, though it sprung from its neglect. Englishmen at home armed themselves because the Governments had not provided for the defence of the United Kingdom; Englishmen abroad followed their example because the same Governments left them "naked to their enemies." Those abroad "will do yeomen's service on their own ground;" those at home will only resist invasion. Between them lie our Imperial water roads, which our fleets cannot protect unless the "strategic points" which command them are efficiently garrisoned in war. The armed Englishmen abroad think it is no affair of theirs, those at home think it is no part of their duty to garrison and defend the keys of the Empire. Colonial Legislatures regard it as an "Imperial responsibility," the British Parliament seems to regard it as a "colonial burden." Meantime, places like Vancouver's, Fiji, King George's Sound, St. Helena, and others are to be left to take care of themselves. Thus, in chasing a "will-o'-the-wisp," composed of imaginary and fantastical distinctions between " colonial burdens " and " Imperial responsibilities," we are walking into a dangerous quagmire, to find, perhaps too late, that there are no such " distinctions " and no separate " burdens," and that with a federal army and a federal fleet we might have defied attack, and thus prevented war.

Our fleets, however, will want other things besides military garrisons at their bases. In these days they will need dockyards near at hand, providing sufficient means of repair; and they will require a sure, steady, and certain supply of coal and telegraphic communication.

To protect the trade lines in the Pacific Ocean, with its 70,000,000 square miles of water, we shall in war require an enormous fleet. That fleet should be entirely independent of Atlantic dockyards, and a great Imperial dockyard at the other side of the world is a most apparent necessity.*

* **Australia.**—" The only proposition of real value . . . . is that England should have a dockyard somewhere in the Pacific."—*Melbourne Leader*, July 28th, 1877.

" The suggestion that the Imperial Government should have a dockyard at Sydney is, of course, one that will meet with no opposition here; and a Bill is now passing through the Imperial Parliament which provides that fortifications in a colony may be vested in the Governor of a colony on behalf of Her Majesty, so that there would be perfect Imperial control over the Imperial property. What the colonists are doing in the way of defence is for their own sakes, and is of course limited by their means and by their necessities. But if any particular port is thought to be of such transcendent importance for the purposes of Imperial strategy that it is not safe to leave it to a limited colonial defence, but that as a matter of Imperial policy it ought to be made

Though Australia and New Zealand are first and chiefly concerned, it is not merely a colonial want. Every portion of our Empire has an interest in that ocean, and therefore such a dockyard is a great Imperial requirement. If it be said our Empire cannot afford to create such a dockyard, then let us quietly haul down the Union Jack in the Pacific before we are ignominiously compelled to strike it. But before doing so, it may be worth considering whether it would not be a better alternative to abolish one of our home dockyards, and remove the officials, plant, and sufficient reserve ships to Sydney, the natural Portsmouth of the Pacific. The loss at home would be more apparent than real. Though there would be one Royal dockyard less at home, the pressure both in peace and war of the maintenance of fleets for half the world

---

absolutely impregnable, then there is nothing to prevent an Imperial protection being superadded to the colonial works."— *The Sydney Morning Herald*, August 4th, 1877.

"A naval arsenal to be complete in itself involves fortifications and a permanent garrison. These also would have to be treated as Imperial."—*The Adelaide Observer*, August 4th, 1877.

"A dual naval base in England and Australia would be of the utmost importance, the establishment of an Imperial dockyard at Sydney being especially desirable. But in considering these questions of strategic necessity and of the distribution of the cost of defence, it must be borne in mind that it cannot be settled off-hand. If, however, Colonel Crossman's calculation is not very far below the mark, that the actual defences of the Empire would not exceed 2,000,000*l*., which could be equitably charged on the Imperial and Colonial Exchequer, then we can at present foresee no great obstacle to the initiation of a practical scheme which would remove the reproach of defencelessness all along our lines of communication."—*The South Australian Advertiser*, August 14th, 1878.

would be removed. The resources of private yards at home are so enormous that not only can they meet the demands of the mercantile marine in its busy time of peace, but they can turn out war vessels, for our possible enemies, by scores. They would be idle in war, and available for the construction and repair of war ships. There are no such private naval resources away from English shores, and therefore at present for aid, for reinforcements, and for maintenance, the enormous Pacific fleet responsible for the safety of half the world must in war rely on private and public yards crowded together in a small island in the north-east corner of the Atlantic ocean! To use a homely phrase, "all our naval eggs are in one basket," and though we may lay them on one side of the globe, the communications on the other may be exposed or shut out from us while they are being hatched.*

There are, however, economical as well as strategical aspects of the question of an Imperial dockyard at Sydney.

1. A ship fitted out in England for the Pacific would be at least two months later on the scene of action than if fitted out at Sydney. The expense of her maintenance during that passage would be

* **New Zealand.**—" Now that the neutral flag is recognized as a protection to cargo, it would not need many losses, nor any long period of paying war premiums, to convince colonial merchants and the people suffering from the larger prices of everything they had to buy and the less of what they had to sell, that this advantage was to be found in independence."—*The Colonist*, August 21st, 1877.

saved. While passing from England to the Pacific or back the vessel cannot be counted as effective force, either in that ocean or at home, and coal consumed would alone add very considerably to her value by the time she reached her destination.

2. The resources of such a dockyard at Sydney would be available in peace for the repair and construction of merchant shipping.

3. The extent of the ocean and the nature of the service to be performed points unmistakably to the conclusion that in war the chief demand to be met will be for swarms of small unarmoured or partially armoured cruisers. Those who have read the admirable paper on "Civilization in the Pacific," * by Mr. Coleman Phillips, and studied Mr. Read's essay, do not require to be told that such vessels can be constructed at Sydney cheaper than in any other part of the world.

4. As we must expect great development in that English mercantile marine having its birthplace and its home in the great Pacific Ocean, so must we prepare to protect it in war. The ties of youth are not easily broken, and a little care and attention to a mercantile marine starting in life may be the means of binding together the interests and the sympathies of our peace and war navies on the other side of the world.

There is a cloud no bigger than a man's hand

* See 'Journal Royal Colonial Institute,' 1875-6.

hovering near Cape Horn; it is a warning for the Empire to " gird itself up and run for the entrance of the gates of Sydney." Developments and civilization are steadily advancing to the South, and we have allowed the coal in the Straits of Magellan to slip through our Imperial fingers. Six miles from Sandy Point a coal mine has been opened and connected by rail with the wharf. " Vegetables of all kinds are grown in abundance, and there is excellent pasture for sheep. The Settlement now to a great extent produces enough to supply itself, and it is to be hoped," says Mr. Rumbold,* " that it will ere long supply the Falkland Islands." Where we have not the command of coal, we shall not in war have the power of military and naval communication. A damaged or worn-out ship must, under our existing arrangements, sail the whole way from Sydney to Plymouth, 13,000 miles, and take chance of falling an easy prey to any small steamer having coal in her bunkers.

The Chinese Empire in the last ten years has converted 117 acres of ground into a dockyard and arsenal, with means and appliances both of construction and repair, quite equal to such as we require for our Pacific fleets. It is rather too much to suppose the English Empire cannot follow in the wake of the Chinese!

When we turn to the Cape, the same arguments

* ' Report on the Progress and General Condition of Chili,' 1875.

apply towards the Imperial necessity of providing naval resources, but they are considerably modified by its proximity to England. The same Imperial reasons for providing adequate means of naval repair and protected coal stores apply to this great strategic point of empire. Powers of construction are not required, but localization and self-reliant support of naval force in that district of ocean are equally necessary. The protection of the road round the Cape is a matter which, though it first and chiefly concerns that colony, is nevertheless a matter in which every portion of the Empire has a vital and direct interest.

The fleet-centres appear to be England for the North Atlantic, Baltic, and Mediterranean, the Cape for the South Atlantic, Bombay for the Indian Ocean, and Sydney for the Pacific. The smaller links of the chain of responsibility which must bind the whole Empire together by defending its lines of communication must not be neglected, remembering that the whole strength is but equal to that of its weakest part. Means of minor repair, stores and coal must be provided at squadron-centres such as St. Helena, Antigua, Mauritius, Singapore, and several other points to which I have elsewhere referred. It is impossible in a short paper, on so huge a subject, to enter into details. They will all require strong garrisons in time of war; many of them have but few English residents, and are but comparatively small worth to trading enterprise. But places of little commercial importance in peace, will be by war suddenly transformed into positions of immense value, to which our helpless merchant shipping will naturally run for shelter, and our exhausted war vessels look for succour and support. If there are no forts and no garrisons, they may seek and look in vain. There is no law of nature which strategically distributes populations, and if we hope to solve the problem of Imperial defence by the simple process of arming residents, we may suddenly find the whole fate of our Empire depending on a corporal's guard, and reap the consequences of adopting a system which has had no place in history, dating from a time when the "four kings" waged the first war in the world, and even these "were joined together in the vale of Siddim which is the salt sea."

It was naval and military combinations saved our Empire in the past. It was the ready unfettered power of combining naval and military force applied by us at the strategic points which brought down to the dust the power of the Dutch. Let us be warned by the lesson of St. Eustatius in 1781. The Dutch power was great in the Spanish Main, their colonies were of immense importance, and their commerce great. War was going on all round them, but true to their purely commercial instincts, they neglected means of defence—it was regarded as unnecessary because they were neutral. The centre of their trade and commerce was the small island of St. Eustatius. They were making money by supplying our enemies, and thus it happened we suddenly declared war on the 21st December, 1780. Instructions were at once sent to our Admiral (Rodney) in those seas "to attack and subdue the possessions of the States General," and saying, "the islands which present themselves as first objects of attacks are St. Eustatius and St. Martin's, neither of which it is supposed are capable of making any considerable resistance." These orders reached the Admiral at Barbadoes 27th January, 1781. He embarked military forces under General Vaughan, and on the 3rd February dropped anchor at St. Eustatius. He gave the Island one hour to surrender, and to use his own words, "the astonishment and surprise of the garrison and inhabitants was scarce to be described." The place instantly surrendered. Thus in an hour not only had the keys of the Dutch position in the West Indies passed into English hands, but also 130 ships besides a Dutch frigate of thirty-eight guns, which was immediately manned by British officers and seamen, and a few days later was cruising against the Dutch and capturing Dutch ships! "Had the

* **Australia.**—"But then the question at issue is one of politics as well as one of military science, and it is our function to look at it from a political point of view; and it appears to us to be inevitable that under the present relations which these colonies maintain with the mother-country, there is no other alternative but that the colonists should defend themselves from aggression and leave the naval charge of the ocean highways to the mother-country."—*Sydney Morning Herald*, August 3rd, 1877.

Dutch," says Rodney, "been as attentive to their security as they were to their profits the Island had been impregnable." Thus was St. Eustatius taken, and with it fell the islands of Saba and St. Martin, and seven weeks later the colonies of Demerara and Essequibo. Now, had the forces of General Vaughan been rooted to Barbadoes, Rodney could not have struck this Imperial blow at the centre of national Dutch power.

We carefully study Napoleon's preparations for invasion, in order to learn how to resist it; we take no notice of his elaborate arrangements for the capture of our strategic points abroad, particularly St. Helena, then strongly garrisoned and defended. So little do we value it now, that though at the outbreak of war with Russia in 1854 a heavy Russian frigate was known to be in the South Atlantic on passage to the Pacific, no official notice that the English Empire was at war was sent to the Government of our most important outpost in that sea.* It is important to remember this in connection with what I have previously stated, viz. that the seizure of St. Helena means the partial investment of the United Kingdom, the lock-out of all our colonies whose lines pass round both Capes, the loss of our command in half the world. Though the United Kingdom is first and chiefly concerned in the defence of St. Helena, every portion of the British Empire is vitally interested in its security.

* I have this on the best authority.

If we do not value such places because they are ours, let us remember what we suffered when they were in an enemy's hands. Take the Mauritius as an example of this. Napoleon recognized the importance of that strategic position, and amply provided for its requirements. De la Bourdonnais, some sixty years before, had developed its resources as a naval base. As a French post it was a thorn in the side of British India and British trade in the East. The Marquis of Wellesley resolved in 1800 to take it, and a military force, 1800 strong, was collected for the purpose at Trincomalee, commanded by Colonel Wellesley, afterwards the Duke of Wellington. It could not go without a naval escort, it was helpless without the fleet, and there it had to wait for Admiral Rainer's squadrons. When they arrived the Admiral objected to the proceedings, and the expedition had therefore to be abandoned.* Now those who think a fleet can go anywhere and do anything without a movable army, or that naval bases can be left unprovided with fortifications and garrisons, should carefully study history. I submit one passage from the secret and private despatch of Marquess Wellesley, 5th February, 1801 : "A naval war of the most

---

* It is worthy of note that in 1794, at Bastia, the same description of administrative difficulty arose, but with the conditions reversed. General Dundas would not do as the Admiral (Hood) and Nelson wished. In this case, however, the navy did what the General "after mature consideration" considered to be impossible. No one, however, was more astonished at the successful result of the naval siege of Bastia than Nelson himself.

destructive nature is now actually waged by the enemy against the commerce of India by the aid of those French Islands, and cannot be terminated without their reduction." It is generally supposed "Trafalgar" effectually settled our supremacy of the sea all over the world, but that is a mistake. The batteries and garrison of this French strategic position enabled the French fleet to defy our naval forces on Indian seas for five long years after that decisive battle was fought. The damage that fleet inflicted on our commerce was almost past calculation. "In 1807," says Beveridge,* "the port of Calcutta alone in six weeks sustained losses by capture to the amount of 300,000*l.*" In 1809 four frigates under Captain Willoughby, with a detachment of the 33rd and 69th regiments, attempted to take Port Louis. We lost all four frigates in the fruitless attempt. They fell a sacrifice to naval and military combination and shore batteries. When the French boarded Captain Willoughby's ship they found nothing but wounded, dead, and dying, and he himself sitting on the capstan, his arm dangling in its socket, his eye hanging on his cheek, singing, "Rule Britannia." † Britannia, however, did not rule in this region for another

* 'History of British India.'
† **New Zealand.**—" Granting all the pride of being part of a mighty Empire, it would speedily give way under the pressure of general distress. A fall in wool and a rise in sugar would appeal irresistibly to the most enthusiastic chanter of 'Rule Britannia.'"—*The Colonist*, August 21st, 1877.

year, when the place was taken by 10,000 troops and eighteen ships of war. These are useful facts to remember in days of free trade, when the wealth of the English race covers the world "as the waters cover the sea." Let the advocates of the simple system of undefended coal ports, dockless and unfortified naval bases, and self-reliant immovable detachments, remember that at present a fillibustering force even can take most of them, and once taken from us we shall have no movable military force available to recapture them, for the moment they are taken they will at once be put in a state of defence. Let it also not be forgotten that even if England and her colonies combine * to fortify and defend them now before it is too late, hornets' nests may still in war be established round Australia, the Cape, and the West Indies, and we

---

* **Australia.**—"We do not wish in any way to defend the doctrines of meanness, or to train the colonists in shirking any part of their fair responsibility, or to ask that the tax-payers in England should bear a burden that fairly devolves on the tax-payers in Australia. But when Captain Colomb lays so much stress on defending ocean highways, and the property that travels thereon, we are forced to ask whether that property does not to an enormously preponderating extent belong to England and not to the colonies. It is true that the ships that run between England and Australia are of equal convenience to us and to our brethren at home, but nearly all the ships belong to England, nearly all the outward cargoes are the speculations of English shippers, and even the homeward cargoes are to a very large extent bought on English account, before they leave our shores. The fact is that the commerce of England is so large that it spreads over all the world and rising communities are more or less mortgaged to English capitalists; and the great English navy exists quite as much for the protection of this commerce as for any other purpose."—*Sydney Morning Herald*, August 2nd, 1877.

must have movable military forces to root out and to destroy them.

It seems to be forgotten that free trade in peace means in war naval armaments of all descriptions and sorts beyond calculation great. We are not and we never can be a great military nation, but if we are to live as an Empire, if we Englishmen are to live at all, we must hold together on the sea. To do so England and her colonies must combine, and the British Empire "grapple to its soul with hoops of steel" the strategic points of power on the sea.

The aggregate annual value of exports and imports of British colonies and possessions is something like 300,000,000*l*. The value of exports and imports of the United Kingdom in 1806 was but some 60,000,000*l*., while last year it was 655,000,000*l*., therefore the colonies alone have five times and we have ten times a greater stake in the sea than we had in the year succeeding Trafalgar. The navy estimates for 1805 were 14,493,843*l*.; in 1814 they were 22,000,000*l*., or a little over one-fourth of the value of our exports and imports of that year. The value of exports and imports of Australian colonies alone is now equal to that of England and France together in 1802 —the year of the peace of Amiens. Such facts as these sufficiently indicate that the burden of protection of our common commerce in war must be shared and justly distributed according to the capacity of the several joints in the Imperial back;* they point unmistakably, first, to federal

* **Australia.**—"The need or even the expediency of a comprehensive system of naval defence for the whole Empire has yet to be demonstrated to Imperial as well as to colonial tax-payers. If conceded, its practicability has next to be proved, and after that the comprehensive plan has to be formed. The final stage, and one apparently still a long way off, will be the question of cost. It was significant that so few colonial statesmen at the meeting entered on the purely political aspect of the case."—*Adelaide Observer*, August 4th, 1877.

"This can only be done by co-operation and the adoption of a joint strategic policy whereby troops could be transferred from one place to another. We are afraid that here, however, the difficulty long foreseen is yet insurmountable, for the very restraints which make the militia and volunteers immovable at home will probably operate to prevent the local armies of these colonies from being sent to Ceylon or Fiji, although they might act in common and at any assailed point for the defence of Australia."—*The South Australian Advertiser*, August 14th, 1877.

Hong Kong.—"There are, of course, few colonies in a position to contribute men like Canada, but in another quarter of a century, probably, Australia, New Zealand, and the Cape will be able to follow her example. In the meantime, most of them can contribute in money, and thus lighten the burden of the mother country. At present many of the colonies defray military contributions, but these are somewhat unequally levied. Ceylon, the Straits Settlements, and Mauritius, which colonies all require a larger garrison for their defence, rightly pay a good round sum for it. Hong Kong also contributes a large amount, one out of all proportion with that of other colonies similarly situated. Malta, for instance, pays about one-sixth of the amount contributed by this colony. The troops located here are intended as much for the defence of the British communities in China and Japan as for that of the island. Yet the residents in the Treaty ports do not bear any of the cost. The contribution would not be unreasonable if it did not fall upon Hong Kong alone. As it is, the residents at Shangai, Yokohama, &c., enjoy a great and unfair advantage. The Hong Kong military contribution clearly ought to be reduced. But the principle that the colonies should help to bear part of the expense incurred in their protection, is undoubtedly correct, and we trust the fact will be spontaneously recognized by them."—*The Daily Press*, Hong Kong, July 23rd, 1877.

Australia.—"The most rigid economist who fairly looks in the face the reasons for the maintenance of the British fleet, and the retention of British naval ports, will admit that if the Australians were

naval positions, and next to a federal fleet and a federal movable army to support that fleet.

If the Empire has deliberately accepted the principle that each portion of it should be independently responsible for its territorial defence, no matter whether the population or internal resources of each are sufficient for the purpose or not, it has accepted a principle which renders it liable in war to subjugation in detail, unless the fallacy be assumed that the fleet of the United Kingdom can everywhere prevent any hostile attack exceeding in power means of isolated local defence. More than this, it risks the command of the sea, without which territorial defence in the United Kingdom means starvation, and in the colonies ruin. I venture to think the colonies have never been asked a question in the matter, and have simply accepted this principle of "domestic defence" because they were left no choice but to adopt it. They are loyal, and they are true, and though they must each and all, except Canada, acknowledge military weakness, they trust implictly to one of two things—first, that war may not come till time has made them strong; second, that if it does come before they are ready,

---

separated to-morrow, England would not on that account maintain one ship the less, or dismantle a single fort, or recall a single garrison."—*Sydney Morning Herald*, August 3rd, 1877.

Bermuda.—"There is a disinclination in the colonies to incur liabilities for military purposes, the immediate necessity of which is not apparent."—*Bermuda Royal Gazette*, June 3rd.

they trust to the statesmen of England to provide for every deficiency, and to cover every defect: they look to them, in short, to do "the rest." Now, it is just these very deficiencies, it is just these very defects; it is, in short, "the rest" of Imperial defence that the statesmen of England cannot provide for without the spontaneous pressure of hearty, willing, and practical co-operation of the colonies. They require watching and urging on, and they would not be human if they did not.

It is most important to remember that in 1854 we drifted into a war wholly unprepared. We declared war, and left "the rest" to the War Office and the Admiralty, and land transport, food, and clothing for our Crimean army were lost in the gulf which lies between the two departments. In that year the Secretary of State for War ceased to be also Secretary for the Colonies, and their affairs passed into the hands of a separate officer of State. It is worthy of note that the requirements of a great war which threatened the colonies rendered it necessary to transfer in 1794 their affairs from the Home Office to the War Department, while the necessities of a smaller war which—as Russia was weak in the Pacific—did not threaten them, caused the care of the colonies to be transferred to an office altogether separate. The next great war will find all matters relating to colonial defence between three stools instead of two. Now, this may account for a good deal of that fog which envelops Imperial defence.

The War Office regards it as chiefly an Admiralty or Colonial Office question: the Admiralty views it as either a War Office or Colonial Office matter; and the Colonial Office, having neither fleets nor armies at its disposal, feels quite certain it only concerns the War Office and Admiralty. The easy way out of the difficulty is to leave each colony to provide for its own defence in any way it thinks fit, and to trust "the rest" to "English pluck" and "English spirit." There is no colonial branch of the Admiralty or War Office, there is no war branch of the Colonial Office, and therefore it is not surprising that every military and naval change has hitherto tended to distort the English vision from taking one wide view of the whole great question; nor should we wonder that Imperial defence has been split up into little bits and strewed about the world.

The people of the United Kingdom would, I believe, spend their last shilling, and fight to their last man, to preserve the Empire intact, and would prepare to do so, and to take their full share of Imperial duty in defence, if they only knew how, if they could only grapple with that "rest," which the colonies look to the statesmen of England to do. Englishmen in the colonies are not different from Englishmen at home, and an Imperial * commission, such as I ventured to suggest ten years ago, and have humbly pleaded for many times since, would let in a flood of Imperial light upon the "parochial" English mind, and let the world know we meant to stick together in defending each other.

It is for Home and Colonial Legislatures, it is for England's sons all over the world to make their voices heard on this matter. We of this generation are the pioneers of the next. When

---

* Cape.—"When, however, such negotiations have been entered, into it will still be questionable who is to pay for the works. Between the Imperial Government and that of the Cape, there will be much more haggling on this question than if the Colonial Parliament had at once voted for such measures of frontier defence as would have shown the Imperial Government that we are quite prepared to undertake the whole of it without the assistance of any British troops."— *Cape Standard and Mail*, July 10th, 1877.

"If ever it should happen to the Imperial Government to take up Captain Colomb's idea of appointing an Imperial Commission to inquire into and report upon the best means of defending the British Empire, we trust the Cape Commissioners will not fail to impress the other Commissioners with the idea that British South Africa is in an exceptional position, and should, while having certain definite claims to Imperial protection, be allowed, to a much larger extent than the other colonies, to shift for herself in all matters connected with defence."— *Ibid.*, June 3rd, 1879.

Australia.—"The appointment of a Royal Commission to examine and report on the best means of defending the outlying parts of the Empire, and apportioning the cost thereof would, we think, be advisable; for then the burden of the expenditure might be so adjusted that little, if any, room for complaint would be left. The only doubt we entertain on this head is whether such an expedient is not too late, though certainly the scheme of independent defence recommended by Sir William Jervois and Colonel Scratchley will hardly militate against the proposals which an Imperial Commission would make."—*The South Australian Advertiser*, August 14th, 1877.

all Europe is an armed camp, and when one single power like Germany, which had but one corvette and two small gunboats in 1848, bids fair to be soon the third great naval power of the world, we cannot go unarmed. We push to the front home and colonial statesmen to warn us of dangers and difficulties ahead; they are the scouts of our history yet to be written, and in days of consolidating power they must not be blind.*

We can hear behind us the measured tread of a host of advancing English nations, whose common path we are to prepare to make plain, and to render safe. We see before us tangled masses of confused systems, which we must do our best to clear away. We are warned of the dangers of our path by the whitened bones of empires which have gone before and perished.

But through the sunshine of peace, or through the darkness and gloom of war, our clear duty and our only hope is still to advance " shoulder to shoulder," helping the weak and cheering on the strong until we have prepared for those who come after us a safe camping-ground on the shores of a

* **Australia.**—"The Colonial Empire may be in a transition state; we may be passing on towards a dismemberment of the Empire; or we may be working towards an Imperial federation. Some think one, some think the other; some wish one, some wish the other; but while we are as we are, parts of one Empire, and yet unrepresented in its Parliament, we do not see how the colonies can be forced to share in an expenditure over which they have no manner of control."—*Sydney Morning Herald*, August 3rd, 1877.

great future. Then, and not till then, can we take the rest of the weary, confident that so far as in us lies, we have done our part to ensure that our Empire shall remain one and indivisible "till wars have ceased in all the world."

CHAPTER V.

THE NAVAL AND MILITARY RESOURCES OF THE COLONIES.*

IN giving effect to the wish of the Council by reading a paper on this subject, I desire, in the first place, to point out the difficulty which limits the possibility of its full discussion here. Resources—especially of war—must be practically available, capable of actual, if not of immediate, application or development. Now, in our great colonies, which offer the widest field for present inquiry, the possible development or the practical availability of such war resources as they possess rests with their own particular Legislatures. Whether these elements of war-power shall or shall not be developed; whether they shall or shall not be made available; whether, in short, they are or are not in the true sense of the term " resources," are matters for their decision and not for this Institution to discuss. Therefore, the vital essence of the whole subject must here remain untouched. Though it be not legitimate in this place to consider whether those things of which I

* Delivered before the Royal United Service Institution, March 28th, 1879.

am about to speak are or are not therefore really and truly our naval and military " resources," we, as officers of constitutional forces, must not be blind to constitutional facts. Those who turn wistful eyes towards Greater Britain seeking for signs of naval and military help in that future no man can foretell, must not overlook the tangle of difficulties we Englishmen—home and colonial—have made for ourselves in the present. The consolidation, development, or even the bare application of dormant or actual war force stored up in other Englands beyond sea are, from a naval and military point of view, purely theoretical questions based upon a complex variety of political assumptions. The carrying out of practical measures necessary for a common system of defence through the machinery of multitudinous Legislatures differently constituted is another and wholly different stupendous problem, statesmen—of England, Canada, Australasia, and the Cape, &c.—have to face.

In order to bring the subject placed in my hands to such a focus as shall render its brief consideration of the smallest practical value, it is therefore necessary to politically assume much. It must be taken for granted that the colonial naval and military resources—whatever they may be—*are* the *common* heritage and present *common* possession of the whole British race: that they are available, can be developed, and may be applied by a homogeneously constituted State: finally, that these resources are to be regarded practically as factors of one great whole, the value of each factor being relative to its use and adaptability in one common Imperial plan of action in war.

From any other standpoint it would be a simple waste of time to investigate the present sources of resisting power—as regards external defence—of any one colony taken by itself, for none isolated and alone could withstand the organized attack of any first-class power. Volumes might be, indeed have been, written respecting the direct defence of the Canadian boundary, but the supporting strength of England is vital to the whole question. Any one of the rich, prosperous, and great colonies in the South Pacific might—under their present arrangement, and if single-handed—suffer severely from armed strength possessed even by such disorganized countries as Chili or Peru. The Cape could not, unaided, stand against the fleet and army of Brazil. Plainly, therefore, the naval and military resources of the colonies can only be practically and usefully considered as component parts of our great Imperial system. The object to be attained by that system being the security in war of the integrity of the dominions of the Queen, and the preservation of the manifold interests of the two hundred millions of human beings Her Majesty—by various Parliaments, Houses of Assembly, and Councils—rules.

I thus introduce the subject because, having been fortunate enough to have elicited discussions in the press of the various colonies, and having closely studied these and the opinions of eminent colonial authorities, relative to Imperial defence, I feel bound to express my conviction that no good and much harm may come of discussing this question concerning the colonies without close regard to their constitutional status.

It is therefore due to this Institution to offer these preliminary remarks, and by doing so I hope to have made what is passing in my mind sufficiently clear without overstepping its laws.

Introductory.

Colonies may be divided into three classes :—

1. Colonies Proper—Agricultural, Pastoral, and Mining; such as Canada, Australasia, and the Cape.

2. Plantation Colonies—such as the West Indies, Ceylon, and Mauritius.

3. Military or trading settlements—such, for example, as Cyprus and the Fijis, Bermuda and the Straits Settlements, Malta and the Falkland Isles, &c., &c.

Of these classes the first demands closest attention, for, as Heenan says, " the colonists who form them become in process of time a nation properly so called."

Naval and military resources may be grouped

under two heads, "raw and developed." Men, for example, are "raw materials," but the trained seaman and disciplined soldier are "developed resources." Coal and iron are "raw materials," the ironclad the perfect product of their development. It is therefore necessary to examine the nature of the raw materials before entering on questions of their present or possible future development.

Raw and developed war resources may each be divided into two branches of inquiry—men and material. The power of any people to preserve by force their own possessions and their own freedom is a question of relative numbers and distinctive characteristics of races. The possession of material resources, however great, may in war prove a curse instead of a blessing to any people too numerically weak, or too numerously neglectful, to prepare to turn them readily to organized account for purposes of self-preservation. Hence the second place—under each head—is here given to material resources. Considerations concerning naval and military resources of the colonies I therefore take in the foregoing order, and venture to remind you it is impossible to do more than hastily point to the most prominent features of so huge a subject.

MEN.

Table I. shows the distribution of population in Colonies Proper.* It will be seen that the aggregate population of the three great groups of colonies is about eight millions, but the value of the war resources, apparently offered by these figures, must be qualified by reference to the various races swelling the total. The Aborigines of New Zealand are not included, nor have I taken account of the 100,000 Indians in Canada, nor of the 30,000 Chinese computed to have recently settled down at the gold-fields of Queensland. Without, therefore, taking these into account, it will be seen that from the total aggregate population I have named, some one and a half million must be deducted. I produce this offset of one and a half million from the total apparent numerical resources, not as a precise statistical statement, but as a fair substantial protest against forming hasty conclusions as to military colonial resources from figures only. Besides non-Europeans so deducted, it must also be borne in mind that the German element in the colonies is considerable, and that a German, until a naturalized British subject, can hardly be counted as a raw material of British war resources.

* The tables concerning the colonies must not be accepted as perfectly accurate, though some trouble to make them sufficiently correct has been taken. A careful examination of and comparison between the various sources of published information, home and colonial, will show the difficulties of obtaining perfect accuracy at present.

NAVAL AND MILITARY RESOURCES OF COLONIES. 163

TABLE No. I.

Colonies Proper.

Group.	Subdivisions.	Area. Square Miles.	Group Area. Square Miles.	Population 1876.	Group Population.	Non-European Population.	Group Non-European Population.
Canada	Dominion	3,372,490	3,412,490	3,686,096*	3,847,470	44,531*	45,151
	Newfoundland	40,000		161,374‡		620‡	
Australasia	New South Wales	323,437	3,173,310	629,776	2,401,715	19,219*	86,797
	Victoria	88,198		840,300		34,858*	
	South Australia	903,690		213,271		..†	
	West Australia	1,057,250		26,709		102	
	Tasmania	26,215		105,484		2,184	
	New Zealand	105,000		399,075		13,285	
	Queensland	669,520		187,100		17,149	
Cape	Cape Colony	199,950	366,605	720,984	1,745,674	484,201	1,424,960
	British Kaffraria	3,463		86,201		86,201	
	Basutoland	8,450		127,700		127,700?	
	Fingoland and Nomansland	5,000		140,000		140,000	
	Griqualand W.	16,632		45,277		20,000	
	Transvaal	114,360		300,000		264,000	
	Natal	18,750		325,512		302,858	
	Totals	..	..	..	7,994,859	..	1,556,908

* Census 1871.   † No Returns.   ‡ Census 1875.

It is obviously impossible to enter further into details, but I would point out that, after making reasonable deductions, the aggregate resources offered by British population of the three great groups of Colonies Proper—*if estimated by numbers*—are more than three times those of Denmark, nearly double those of Portugal, and greater than those of Belgium. Canada in this respect bears fair comparison with the Netherlands, and Australasia with Switzerland. The ratio of increase of population of our colonies cannot, however, be compared to any country of the Old World; Canada's population, for example, has increased some sevenfold in fifty years, and about doubled within the last five-and-twenty years. The aggregate population of colonies in Australasia has more than doubled in the last sixteen years, and is now about seventeen times what it was when Her Majesty began to reign.

It must not, however, be forgotten that numerical strength of population is—as an element of war resources—directly affected by reference to the territorial area over which it is distributed. Now there are some 389 persons to every square mile in England and Wales, while in Australasian colonies, the most densely populated, Victoria, has but 10 to the square mile; and the least, Western Australia, but *one individual to every* 38 *square miles*.

In Canada, a population about equal to that of

London is distributed over an area half as big again as that of Russia in Europe.

In viewing population as a raw material of war resources, it is to be observed that emigration from these islands to a foreign territory represents so much present loss of war-power to us, and an incalculable increasing gain of war-power in the future to a possible enemy.* The transfer of population from one part of the Empire to another merely varies the distribution of this element of strength, and such redistribution may, if utilized, be of inestimable military benefit in war. The pale-faced artisan, born, bred, and working in the fœtid atmosphere of an overcrowded manufacturing town at home, is a very inferior " raw material " of war resources—to the hardy Englishman labouring by the shores of Winnipeg, the banks of the Murray or the Clutha, or on his "claim" in Griqualand West. The historian Froude has so eloquently and forcibly written on this subject that further general remark is needless. Some very striking passages from his 'Short Studies on Great Subjects' will be found quoted in Mr.

* During the twenty-five years ending 31st December, 1877, upwards of 4,000,000 persons (of British origin) emigrated from the United Kingdom, of which 2,700,000—a number greater than the present total population of Switzerland—went to the United States. In 1877 the emigration was as follows:—
 45,000 to the United States.
 30,000 to Australia.
 7,000 to Canada.
 11,000 to all other places.
These figures are in round numbers for illustration of principles.

Brassey's paper in the Journal of this Institution. It is, however, proper here to call attention to the opinion of a military authority. "The Canadians possess," says Lieutenant-General Sir Selby Smyth, "in a marked degree, qualities to make excellent soldiers, being both hardy and industrious, used to rough life, easily subjected to discipline, and willing to submit to necessary authority. . . . . There are no better soldiers than Canada can produce." Turning our eyes towards these islands, it must be acknowledged that manufacturing progress at home is rapidly absorbing rural populations, and shrinking the recruiting area which, from natural causes, provides the best raw material of military force. It is calculated our home population will amount in seventy-six years from this to some sixty millions, nearly double what it is now. We may therefore expect the quality of raw material yearly offered by home recruiting fields to diminish rather than to increase with numbers; while in our colonies it is both in quantity and quality increasing every year at a rate difficult to accurately estimate. It has, however, been calculated that, in some twenty-one years from this date, the aggregate population of Canada, Australasia, and the Cape will be some fifteen millions, nearly half what the total population of the United Kingdom is now—about equal to what it was at the date of Waterloo.

Before, therefore, the Naval Cadet of to-day is

an Admiral; before the Sandhurst Cadet of to-day is a General Officer Commanding, colonial population will form numerically a very substantial proportion of British war resources, and probably be superior in quality to that likely then to be furnished by the mother-country. The true value and availability, therefore, of this element of national war strength lies—as regards these colonies —more in the immediate future than in the actual present; but, forasmuch as it takes at least a whole generation to build up a national, naval, or military organization, it is full time now to begin to lay the foundation of such a truly national system as shall embrace all the products of these British developments, and have for its object the welding together of the elements of English war strength into "one harmonious whole." It appears to me that a system which now does not do so, must, in a generation, be discarded as effete and obsolete, or remain—to produce gradual but certain disintegration of English war-power by excluding from its original sources of naval and military strength the more vigorous portions of our race.

Questions concerning the raw materials of war resources, offered by the subject races in Canada and at the Cape, should properly here be considered. It is, however, too special a subject to introduce incidentally. Such resources, whatever their true value, must ever be secondary to those furnished by British blood. Those at the Cape can only be fairly estimated when the present war is closed. In Canada the proportion of native races to British is very small, but it may be fitting here to quote from an Address to the Queen from the Chiefs of the Six Nations, "assembled at their council fire," during the Crimean War. "Great Mother," they wrote, "your children of the Six Nations have always been faithful and active allies of your Crown, and the ancestors of your Red children never failed to assist in the battles of your illustrious ancestors."

On the general questions relative to the Imperial availability of military resources furnished by native populations, I would venture to remark that the truth—as it generally does—would appear to lie between two extreme opinions. The one which describes a contingent of Her Majesty's Native troops commanded by distinguished British officers as a "horde of savages" is not worthy of scientific consideration, but the other extreme of opinion may become a source of real danger. It appears to be briefly this: that "Home defence" is one thing, and "Imperial defence" another; that so long as British pockets are full, a sufficiency of "billets for bullets" on distant battle-fields can always be readily procured, and may be chiefly furnished by the bodies of British subjects having a darker coloured skin. But if the teachings of history are to be trusted, this peace philosophy, based upon the sandy foundations of money and subject races, will not, in time of trouble, avail us much. The signal at Trafalgar was surely not of momentary import, but for all time the Shibboleth of safety of England and her colonies alike.

Table II. shows approximately the distribution of population in plantation colonies. It will be seen that the war resources offered by white population are of little *numerical* practical value. Climatic and other influences combine to render it improbable that this element can ever be in *this particular respect* of much account.

Table III. gives similar information concerning military and trading settlements, to which the same remark applies generally with greater force.

Raw Resources, Material.

Out of innumerable materials necessary for Naval and Military purposes, it may here suffice to select three: Food, coal, and horses.

Food.

It must be remembered we are now considering colonial Naval and Military resources as component parts of one great whole, of which the United Kingdom is the citadel. It is, therefore, of great naval and military importance to understand how that citadel is provisioned, and how far colonial resources are capable of supplying its wants.

TABLE No. II.

PLANTATION COLONIES.

Group.	Colony.	Area. Square Miles.	Group Area. Square Miles.	Population 1876.	Group Population.	European Population.	Group European Population.
West Indies	Bahamas	5,390	96,351	39,162	1,279,091	6,500	68,190
	Guiana	76,000		193,491		15,000*	
	Honduras	7,562		24,710		377	
	Jamaica and Turk's Isle	4,193		506,154		13,101	
	Leeward Isles	655		4,723		272	
	Windward Isles	797		117,583		5,886*	
	Trinidad	1,754		283,630		22,054*	
				109,638		5,000*	
Eastern	Mauritius	713	25,415	329,754	2,735,041	108,534	126,816
	Ceylon	24,702		2,405,287		18,282	
	Totals	..	121,766	..	4,014,132	..	195,006

* There being no official returns distinguishing white from coloured population, these figures are taken from a table compiled by Dr. J. Forbes Watson.

TABLE No. III.
MILITARY AND TRADING SETTLEMENTS.

Imperial Line.	Station.	Area. Square Miles.	Group Area. Square Miles.	Population.	Group Population.	European Population.	Group European Population.
Canadian							
Canada and West Indian	Bermudas	19	19	..	12,121	..	4,725
Australasian, viâ Suez	Gibraltar	1¾		20,936			
	Malta	119		141,918			
	Cyprus	2,288	2,420	14,764	200,336		
	Perim	7		211			
	Aden	5		22,507			
China Extension	Straits Settlements	1,445		308,097		209	209
	Labuan	30	1,506	4,898	437,193	1,730	9,305
	Hong Kong	31		124,198	7,525		
Australasian and Canadian	Fijis	..	7,403	..	142,000	..	1,683
Cape	W. Africa { Gambia	69		14,190		57	
	Branch { Sierra Leone	463		37,089		107	
	Gold Coast	6,000	6,691	408,070	527,638	70	5,545
	Lagos	73		62,021		94	
	Ascension	34		27		27	
	St. Helena	47		6,241		5,190	
Cape and Aden	Seychelles	..	..	13,095	..	?	..
Cape and Australasian							
Australasian, viâ Cape Horn	Falkland Isles	..	6,500	..	1,114	..	1,110
	Totals	..	..	..	1,320,402	..	22,815

According to the elaborate calculations of Mr. S. Bourne, it appears "that out of thirty-three million inhabitants of the United Kingdom, eighteen millions may be sustained on food grown at home, and fifteen millions on that received from abroad."* He further points out, "on an average, each member of the community now consumes to the value of two and a half times as much foreign food as he did twenty years back."

It is just ten years ago since in two lectures † here I endeavoured to show the extreme danger of limiting the military scope of National Defence simply to these islands. The aim of those papers was to draw attention to a disagreeable, and *then* most unpopular truth, viz., that military arrangements for *even a passive* defence could not be confined to the simple question of invasion, because without military aid abroad for our fleets to rest upon, the safety of our water-roads was imperilled, and unless these communications were secured absolutely, we could be—starved out. The defence of our Imperial communications, be it remembered, is not a purely Naval question, but a very complex problem involving a great variety of Naval and purely Military considerations.‡ The national necessity for no longer delaying to deal with it is

* *Vide* paper read before the Manchester Statistical Society, "On the Increasing Dependence of this Country on Foreign Supplies of Food." By Mr. S. Bourne, F.S.S., 1877.

† "Distribution of our War Forces," Journal, vol. xiii., No. 53.

‡ If the Naval Prize Essay, 1878, Captain P. H. Colomb, R.N., Journal, vol. xxii., No. 94, be read in conjunction with "Strategic

increasing with marvellous rapidity. At the date, 1869, these papers here referred to were read, the value of the chief articles of food per head of population imported was at the rate of 37 *shillings and five pence* per annum, while by 1877 it had risen gradually to 57 *shillings and seven pence*. The food required by fifteen thirty-thirds of our home population at present comes from various countries of the world; consequently we have a great variety of divergent supply lines. Our Imperial connecting lines must be defended irrespective of all other considerations, and if our colonies possessed food resources requisite to supply home wants, our food lines and our Imperial lines could, in war, become identical. So far, therefore, as the actual sustentation of our people at home is concerned, this would be equivalent to an increase of war strength; hence the close connection between colonial food and Naval and Military resources.

Table IV. illustrates the imports of food into the United Kingdom in 1877. It sufficiently exhibits the truth that we are not, as regards food, a self-supporting Empire. This is a great Naval and Military fact, and one on which the whole question of a real national policy of defence turns. It would be impossible here to push inquiry below

Harbours," General Collinson, R.E., Journal, vol. xviii., No. 77, and Pasley's 'Military Policy and Institution of the British Empire,' 1808, the complexity and gravity of the question will be fully understood. See Appendices 1 and 2.

TABLE No. IV.
FOOD.

Abstract Table showing principal Articles of Food imported into the United Kingdom 1877, distinguishing, as far as possible, those from India, the Colonies, and Foreign Countries.

Nature of Food.	India.	Colonies.	Foreign.	Countries not specified, &c.	Total.
LIVING ANIMALS (NUMBER).					
Live animals	..	18,495	1,045,949	30,838	1,095,282
MEAT, FISH, GRAIN, MEAL, AND FLOUR. RICE, BUTTER, CHEESE, AND POTATOES, IN CWTS.					
Meat and fish	..	520,757	4,917,228	35,719	5,473,704 cwts.
Grain, meal, and flour	6,103,585	7,363,595	110,761,828	399,185	124,628,193 "
Rice	6,251,074	..	293,578	72,951	6,617,603 "
Butter, cheese, and potatoes ..	..	418,403	10,440,528	397,232	11,256,163 "
Total cwts.	12,354,659	8,302,755	126,413,162	905,087	147,975,663 cwts.
TEA, COFFEE, SUGAR, AND COCOA.					
Tea, lbs.	30,940,724	..	156,464,403	110,157	187,515,284 lbs.
Coffee, cwts.	159,932	894,391	549,918	4,041	1,608,282 cwts.
Sugar, cwts.	891,013	5,091,978	14,047,260	20,546	20,050,797 "
Cocoa, lbs.	..	8,171,088	8,871,115	14,161	17,056,364 lbs.

the figures of that table, but in order to explain its illustrative importance, brief further remarks may be useful.

Taking wheat, for example, we imported during 1877 fifty-four and a quarter million odd *hundredweights*. Of this, some forty-four and three-quarter million *hundredweights* came from some fifteen different foreign countries, but ·nine and a half million *hundredweights* came from our own possessions. Of this nine and a half millions, some six millions came from India, and three and a half millions from the colonies. It is to be observed that of the total wheat required by these two islands in 1877, only about one-ninth came from India—probably less through the Suez Canal—and only about one-seventeenth of the whole was furnished by the colonies. We had, during that year, some eighteen different wheat supply lines, made up as follows: fifteen from foreign countries, one from India, one from Canada, and one from Australasia. The great bulk, therefore, of the staple article of our food travelled in 1877 along lines by no means identical with the connecting lines of our Empire. The food-producing resources of the colonies are consequently of great Naval and Military importance. What they are it is unnecessary, perhaps, to remind you. Travellers in Canada, Australasia, or the Cape see one common thing, they have but one tale to tell, unlimited food-producing resources belonging to the English race—lying waste. One of the inestimable Naval and Military benefits certain to arise from a natural redistribution of British populations—within the limits of their own Empire—is therefore briefly this, a diminution in the future of the number of food lines absolutely requiring protection in war. The value and availability, however, of colonial food resources—inexhaustible though they be—lies, as a Naval and Military question, more in the future than in the present. They will increase relatively with the first element of war strength—population.*

COAL.

As a preface to remarks on colonial coal, it is proper to say that they are necessarily cursory and confined to an infinitesimal portion of a great subject. Hence it is that no mention is made of some prodigious deposits, some recently discovered, others not yet much worked, in several colonies. This paper is simply illustrative; closer and more adequate examination would directly concern colonies not here mentioned, but nevertheless possessing such wealth.†

* A great variety of interesting and instructive matter, particularly concerning plantation colonies and military and trading settlements, is necessarily left untouched for want of space.

† A very excellent paper, "On the Natural Distribution of Coal throughout the British Empire," was read before the Royal Colonial Institute by the *late* Mr. Eddy, 1872. Though the interval of time elapsed since it was read has altered the complexion of some of the facts, it is still, nevertheless, a valuable guide to a study of the subject.

Coal is not merely a naval resource. Combinations and concentrations of our purely military forces are helplessly dependent on its supply. Before English soldiers could cross the Prah, for example, they had to cross the sea; and this preliminary movement of a small military expedition caused a variation in the export of British coal. The King of Coomassie was probably not aware that a light applied by even one unarmed man to a black mass at a distant Portuguese island would do more to delay the advance of his enemies than the muster at home of all his military hosts; nor did Zulu chieftains at Rorke's Drift know that the time of attack of a reinforced British army might be more or less directly influenced by the coal-carrying capacity and coal consumption of ships selected as transports, or the quantity of fuel stored, and coaling arrangements at that same remote island or St. Vincent. Savages cannot be expected to know these things, but the English executive, Home and Colonial, will for once make a mistake if it expects the Moltkes or Todlebens of future wars to possess—in this matter—only the military intelligence of savages. The close connection between coal and our military movements is sufficiently indicated by the fact that in 1872 our export of coal to Madeira was less than 36,000 tons, to Cape Coast Castle 42 tons; while the year of the expedition, 1873, it was to Madeira over 46,000 tons, to Cape Coast Castle over 3600 tons. If, then, the sending abroad during a time of profound naval peace of a small, compact military force—to punish a barbarous king—involved a variation of distribution of some 14,000 tons of British coal, how great will be the strain on our power of protecting and furnishing coal supplies and coal transport from England when at war with a first-class, and perhaps attacking power! Colonial coal resources will then afford the only means of escape from an unworkable centralization system on a huge scale. According as we have in peace utilized, developed, and prepared to guard them, so shall our Empire in war win the reward of intelligent forethought, or reap the bitter consequences of a stupid neglect.

Turn to the Dominion of Canada, with the Arctic regions in its rear, and along the whole length of its front a power of infinite resources. The United States at the commencement of this century had a white population one-third less than the present aggregate of our colonies proper. Its present population now exceeds the aggregate of the United Kingdom and these colonies together, and it is now the second maritime power in the world. It is, for naval and military purposes, homogeneous, for its central Government can draw on and immediately apply every element of war-power found under its flag. Its left flank rests on the Pacific, and could be turned by sea from the province of British Columbia; its right flank, resting on the Atlantic, could be turned by sea from the province of Nova Scotia, and in its rear are the British West Indies. The combined naval and military operation of turning either flank, or attacking its rear, would primarily be a question of coal, and it is in these two provinces the Great Dominion finds its chief supply.* It would be impossible to enter into any examination here of the relative qualities of coal in the several colonies or parts of colonies. These points will no doubt be dealt with in the discussion which is to follow. I should, however, mention that space compels me merely to touch upon colonial coal actually used now in any quantity by steamers on the sea. San Francisco steamers are largely supplied from British Columbia, while Nova Scotia furnishes some of our own steam lines, the "Allan" for example—with coal, besides exporting it to the States. I now ask you to cross, in imagination, by the Fijis from British Columbia to Australia; passing by Queensland—with its great coal deposits waiting the hour of their full development—we arrive at Sydney. We are now in a colony possessing a coal area of some 24,000 square miles in extent. At Newcastle, 75 miles up the coast, colliers will be found loading for various parts of the world. At San Francisco, Hong Kong, Singapore, and

* Large coal deposits have recently been discovered in the Northwest Territory, near the line proposed for the Pacific Railway, which would connect Halifax with Esquimalt.

Galle, &c., their cargoes will be landed, and mingle with the coal of the mother-country, thus completing the black girdle with which British industry encircles the world. These laden vessels will, in war, be valuable prizes for hostile cruisers, and they will then require either armaments or escorts; still more will it be necessary to guard the sources of coal supply, and to arm and garrison those British points where coal is stored. Our colonies, with their mother-country depending on the agency of coal for nearly all that makes them prosperous in peace, may fairly share with her—in just proportion—the honour and duty of its protection in war. Neither can hope successfully to secure its safety without painstaking preparation during peace. The mother-country cannot justly chide her children for heedless disregard, natural to youth, of a duty which she in her age neglects—as testified by unprotected British coal heaps scattered about the world. Time forbids special reference to other Australasian coal resources, such, for example, as those of Victoria, Tasmania, &c., or those of New Zealand, offering as they do, pledges of that "great maritime future," of which Sir Julius Vogel so eloquently speaks. Passing on our homeward way by the Mauritius to the Cape, we find a vast British territory, the mineral resources of which have not yet been so fully investigated as to warrant practical naval and military conclusions. We cannot, therefore, stop to inquire about the coal deposits in the Stromberg Mountains, Cape Colony; the Highveldt of the Transvaal, or at Biggarsberg, Natal. It is, however, at the present time, fitting to remark that our comrades advancing northward into the heart of Zululand are carrying the banner of St. George towards the Zambesi coal discovered by Livingstone. In our plantation colonies, there is no coal of present naval and military value.* Some, however, of these places like military and trading settlements, are of immense Imperial importance as store supply depôts. Some particulars as to the rapid increase of British coal exports will be seen in Table V. To conclude this rude outline of colonial coal resources, it may be observed that their naval and military value as regards Canada and Australasia lies in the present, and as regards the Cape, in a possible future. Canada and Australasia furnish the British race with the means of providing for its naval and military wants now—and in the future—in regions most remote from home supplies. How far we avail ourselves of them for naval and military purposes is altogether another question. To what extent we are preparing to make our war fleets—or the links in the distant chain of our Imperial communications on which those fleets *must* rest—depend on these natural

* Labuan is an exception; but so many questions of detail would have to be raised concerning Labuan coal, that, in dealing with great principles, it seemed wiser to defer remarks.

TABLE No. V.

Comparative Statement showing Export of British Coal, distinguishing Home and Colonial, from 1854 to 1877 inclusive.

Year.	New South Wales. Exports.	Canada. Exports.	Total Colonial.	United Kingdom. Export.	Total Export. Home and Colonial.
	tons	tons	tons	tons*	tons
1854	59,297			4,309,255	
1855	61,484			4,976,902	
1856	84,086			5,879,779	
1857	96,565			6,737,718	
1858	113,618			6,529,483	
1859	174,195			7,006,949	
1860	233,877	Returns not given in Statistical Abstracts.		7,321,832	
1861	207,904			7,855,115	
1862	308,782			8,301,852	
1863	298,337			8,275,212	
1864	372,601			8,809,908	
1865	383.270			9,170,477	
1866	541,215			10,137,260	
1867	473,666			10,565,829	
1868	548,187			10,967,062	
1869	505,795			10,774,945	
1870	578,564			11,702,649	
1871	565,782			12,747,989	
1872	670,802	322,283	903,085	13,198,494	14,191,579
1873	774,029	404,757	1,178,786	12,617,566	13,796,352
1874	874,143	418,357	1,292,500	13,908,958	15,201,458
1875	928,358	288,176	1,216,534	14,475,036	15,691,570
1876	870,653	284,279	1,154,932	16,255,839	17,410,771
1877	915,727	249,536	1,165,263	14,880,899	16,046,162

* This column is taken from a statement in 'Coal; its History and Uses.'

sources of supply, are matters upon which I shall not now enter; but instead will conclude with two slight illustrations.

So far back as 1877, Mr. Donald Currie, in his lecture here, forewarned the country what might happen in a European war, through the absence of a submarine telegraph to the Cape. At this moment a savage, without even a big boat, has given the greatest "maritime nation in the world" a small taste of the consequence of neglecting such practical views as were then put forth by Mr. Currie. Now it is from that lecture I extract the following pregnant sentence: "It was only a short time ago that the Admiralty inquired how much coal we could spare at the Cape, and whether our fleet could be supplied there, and it was impossible for the Government to learn in less than fifty days their exact position." This, then, is one picture; in the foreground a Government in a seven weeks' ignorance as to the power of locomotion of the national fleet; and in the far distance, that fleet—in waters of Imperial strategic importance,* trusting to a combination of luck and private surplus stores for its coal.

To look at the picture in another light, it is necessary to remember what Mr. Robinson, member of the Natal Legislature, said in this theatre: " There exists in the part of South Africa to which I belong, as fine a field of steam coal as exists in any part of the world. That coal-field is 180 miles from the coast, and we are only too anxious to get communication by railway, but, unfortunately, our poverty and our smallness bar the way. If the Home Government would co-operate with us to connect that coal-field with the sea, it would open out to the British Empire a permanent and good supply of steam coal." †

* The total commerce passing round the Cape, estimated by Lord Carnarvon at 160,000,000*l.* per annum.

† At Camdeboo, some 50 miles from Port Elizabeth, there is also coal of good quality.

In speaking from this place two years ago,[*] I drew particular notice to the defenceless state of our coal depôt at Hong Kong. Since that time circumstances drew special attention to that part of the world. England woke up, thinking a war was close, and hasty preparations were made. Through the indefatigable exertions of two officers defensive works were erected in an incredibly short space of time for the protection of this particular coal depôt. I am neither aware as to whether these works are sufficiently armed, nor whether the artillery force was sufficient to man them, but it is desirable to point out that Hong Kong is only one of a certain number of strategically placed Imperial coal depôts essential to our naval and military power of defence. In the same paper this sentence occurs : " If war breaks out to-morrow, it would find our fleets without any system by which their supply of coal would be assured." I venture to repeat those words again, and do so with the more confidence, because in this very theatre one year afterwards they were fortuitously, yet absolutely, corroborated by the distinguished admiral who, at the time these words were spoken, was commanding the British fleet in the quarter of the world to which they referred. Last year, Admiral Ryder incidentally said : " I have just come from the command on the Japan and China station, and with an imminent prospect

[*] "Russian Development, and our Naval and Military Position in the North Pacific," Journal, vol. xxi., No. 91.

of war, I felt very doubtful whether I should ever get a pound of coal without taking it forcibly from a neutral."

Now my other illustration is this: During the year an admiral " in command " of a British fleet, in Chinese waters, " with an imminent prospect of war," was doubtful as to getting a *pound* of coal,— the total export of coal from Canada and Australia exceeded a million tons, and at Newcastle, New South Wales, hydraulic appliances for rapidly shipping coal had been established at a cost of some 25,000*l.* to the colony.

Some further information respecting exports of British coal will be found in Table VI., and in conclusion I would commend to your special attention the following brief extract from a work called ' Coal; its History and Uses,' by Professors Green, Miall, Thorpe, Rüker, and Marshall. " This country's fortunes," they say, " are gradually being merged in those of a greater Britain, which, largely through the aid of the coal whose prospective loss we are lamenting, has grown beyond the limits of these islands to overspread the vastest and richest regions of the earth." *

* The wealth of iron and other minerals of the colonies is a great naval and military resource. Where iron and coal are found together in large quantities, as in New South Wales and the province of Nova Scotia or British Columbia, and in other colonies, the raw material resources of war are enormous. It was impossible, however, in a short paper to treat of these and many other interesting fields of inquiry. The inestimable benefit sure to arise from the attraction of population from the *one* old part of the Empire to many new branches of it, is the development of these material resources here left untouched.

TABLE No. VI.

Showing Destination of British Coal, in Tons, Exported in 1877.

From	Channel Isles, &c.	India.	Colonies Proper.	Plantation Colonies.	Military and Trading Settlements.	Foreign Countries.	Total.
United Kingdom	66,550	562,376	239,395	285,366	907,944	12,819,268	tons 14,880,899
New South Wales	..	24,629	563,757	4,789	93,388	229,164	915,727
Canada	..	..	47,321	2,295	..	199,920	249,536
Total	66,550	587,005	850,473	292,450	1,001,332	..	..
Grand Total			2,797,810			13,248,352	16,046,162

Horses.

Turning from the agency on which war combinations over sea depend, means of transport for land operations naturally suggests itself for consideration.

It is fitting first to remind you that the prize of 5000 roubles offered by the Czar for the best 'History of Cavalry from the Earliest Times,' was gallantly won by Canada, in the person of Lieutenant-Colonel George T. Dennison, Commanding the Governor-General's Body Guard, author of 'A Treatise on Modern Cavalry,' and spoken of in Lieutenant-General Sir Selby Smyth's Official Report as one "among many excellent cavalry officers of the Dominion."

The war resources of the colonies in "horses" is, I think, a question of immense importance. Armies in Europe are growing almost faster than horses fit for service are bred, and the number of horses required for war purposes increases in direct ratio to force to be placed in the field. A declaration of war is not exactly the time for a nation to be running about seeking horses for its guns, cavalry, and transport. It is all very well for us to rely on free trade for our profits, and the supply of our national wants in peace; but when rumours of war are in the air, the Continental horse-market becomes, somehow or other, uncommonly "tight."

I remember, at one of our "Autumn Manœuvres,"

watching a regimental transport man struggling with a certain ugly pair of grey brutes, exhibiting a marked objection to a certain hill. There was no mistaking the nationality of the horses; nor was there much difficulty in determining that of the man, for between the vigorous strokes of his whip, this—free from adjectives—was his refrain—" Ye don't even speak English, ye brutes, ye don't!"

Now Table VII. exhibits a fact—which naturally recurred to my memory then—that there are, in other Englands beyond sea, some two million horses* more or less accustomed to English ways, an English tongue, and an English hand. This may appear a theoretical mode of introducing a subject of great gravity, and may seem to infer obliviousness to great sea distances, and the effect on horses of long voyages; in short, to lack the possibility of practical application. I hope, however, that, on reflection, it may not so appear. It was impossible here to inquire into the merits and demerits of various colonial coal; and, for the same reason, the characteristics of colonial horses can form no portion of these remarks. It will, however, be of profit to this Institution—and, through it, to the service—if the discussion elicits information on these points from gentlemen of practical colonial experience.

* The number of horses, returned by occupiers of land, in the United Kingdom, 1878, was 1,927,066. *Vide* Agricultural Returns, 1878.

TABLE No. VII.

Horses.

Group.	Subdivision.	No. of Horses.	Total.	Date of Return, and Remarks.
Canada	Dominion	862,072	866,129	Census 1871, Province of British Columbia not included.
	Newfoundland	4,057		Census 1875.
Australia	New South Wales	366,703	958,982	
	Victoria	194,768		
	South Australia	106,903		
	Western Australia	33,502		
	Tasmania	23,622		Return 1876.
	New Zealand	99,850		Census 1874.
	Queensland	133,625		
Cape	Cape Colony	205,985	205,985	No reliable information.
	British Kaffraria	?		
	Basutoland	35,357	35,357	
	Fingoland and Nomansland	11,723	11,723	
	Griqualand W.	?	..	Ditto.
	Transvaal	?	..	Ditto.
	Natal	22,722	22,722	

NAVAL AND MILITARY RESOURCES OF COLONIES. 189

The first general consideration as to horse resources of the colonies is one of numbers; this, for purposes of illustration, is met by Table VII. It is to be borne in mind, however, that the same observation made respecting the extent of area covered by population applies, though perhaps in a more limited degree, to the "raw material" of war furnished by horses. An example of this truth was indirectly afforded by H.R.H. the Duke of Cambridge with reference to the dispatch of horses to the Cape. In the House of Lords, H.R.H. said: "The reason was obvious. To collect a large number of horses on the spot would take time, and it was necessary that the men should go ready to take the field on landing."

The next general reflection is that as our Colonial Empire contains vast territory in every clime—from the frosty N.W. Province of Canada to the tropical districts in Northern Australia—so are to be found within its limits, horses naturally suited to the purposes of war in any part of the world where British forces may have to operate. I may mention that in Queensland five shillings per head has been sometimes paid for shooting wild horses, in order to clear the "Runs" and to prevent interference with the domesticated animals.

Now as regards sea distances, which is the point on which the practical question of value and availability turns. No student of modern warfare can observe the increasing facilities of transporting live animals in large numbers over long sea distances—which have been created by the push and shove rivalry of peaceful commercial competition—without reflecting how means so afforded can be turned to account in war. To my mind, they furnish to us at once a warning and an encouragement. A warning, because they show that long sea distances do not *in themselves* present insurmountable obstacles to foreign attack; an encouragement, because we have only to *prepare* to avail ourselves of the experiences of peace and to consolidate the Imperial resources we possess—to render our Imperial position at all points practically secure. As a matter of fact the military obstacles apparently presented by long sea distances—in the matter of horses—are theoretical obstacles imagined in peace, which, with good management and arrangement, vanish under pressure of war. In peace, large numbers of Australian horses, and no inconsiderable number of Cape horses, find their way to India, and some time ago British Columbia frequently imported horses from the Sandwich Isles, a distance of some 2400 miles. The mutiny in India compelled our establishment there to draw largely on Australia for horses, and the bustle of their embarkation at great ports like Melbourne and Sydney told the tale of military requirements of war capable of fulfilment from points 5000 miles distant. Recent events in one corner of the world caused a native cavalry force to be moved from India to Malta. Across 4000 miles of sea it came, showing Englishmen—home and colonial—that steam has bridged not only the Channel, but the water distances which separate the various portions of our Empire from the mother-country and from each other; and reminding all, that Empire is not merely something "to be enjoyed" in peace, but that it has to be "maintained" by force in war. Again, cavalry, which six weeks ago was at Hounslow and at Aldershot, is now across the Tugela, 6000 miles away, thus completing a practical illustration of possible reciprocity of duty and obligation between England and her colonies. If we can go to them, they can come to us.

It must be remembered, however, that we are now regarding horses as "raw material" of war-power; the "charger" or "battery horse" is a developed material. The certain change from one to the other is but a matter of time and skill, accomplished by forethought and resulting from care, and therefore these short notes under this head may, I think, be thus summed up. The value of military resources of the colonies, as regards horses, lies in the present, and their availability depends upon the nature and extent of arrangements made in peace, by which alone they can, in war, be turned to organized and instant account.

While we remember that cavalry has been rapidly

moved from England to the Cape, and swiftly from Bombay to Malta, let us not forget that there are in Canada, for example, nearly a million horses and "many excellent cavalry officers;" that Ottawa is *nearer* Constantinople than London is to Pietermaritzburg, and that Bombay is *farther* from Malta than Malta is from Halifax.

It is now time to close this rude survey of those "raw materials" of colonial naval and military power which appeared to me most worthy of selection for these short remarks. Whether you agree with me in the general conclusions I have thus far attempted to indicate, or whether you do not, you will not, I hope, at all events be disposed to differ with the following general conclusions. That from a naval and military point of view, the application to any Imperial purpose of such outlying sources of war-power as the colonies possess rests practically on means of transport and the ensured safety of the sea. The colonial mercantile marine may fairly claim its place therefore under the head of "developed resources," and, with the armed strength and naval and military organization of the several colonies, will form subjects for separate consideration.

Brief, and entirely inadequate though these references to the raw material of colonial war-power may be, they form a necessary introduction to the consideration of such developed naval and military resources as the colonies possess. They will, I trust, not be without some slight value. Their very insufficiency will, at all events, show that beneath the surface, over which we have so lightly passed, are yet unfathomed depths of useful study. Great as the natural advantages of England have been in the past, great though they still be in the present, they seem but shrivelled and stunted when compared with those of Greater Britain. Whether the power of self-preservation derivable from such aids will, in days to come, split into fragments, or become united and consolidated, must more or less depend upon the direction of present progress. Either result will more probably be developed from gradual growth, rather than spring from spontaneous or sudden change. If colonial resources, as they become available, are not grafted into one great defensive system for a common purpose and a common good, then our Imperial power of resistance already contains elements of naval and military disintegration, and lacks that unity which is strength.

I cannot, therefore, conclude this portion of my subject without reference to one or two facts which afford some indications of the direction of present progress, and I shall take the heads of this paper in inverse order.

As regards Horses. In 1873, a Committee of the House of Lords inquired into the question of horse supplies. It was stated to the Committee, that "in case of emergency arising, the Continent would be virtually closed to us for the purchase of horses." In reply to the 1643rd question, Canada was referred to as "another country where we could get horses," but which had not been mentioned. Out of 4075 questions, only 33 had reference to Canada; but one witness—Colonel Jenyns—was examined as to Canadian horses. He stated that "they were wonderfully good horses . . . as good troopers as he ever saw," and that "they stand a great amount of hard work and exposure." He was asked would he bring them over in *sailing or steam vessels!!* There is no mention of Canada or of any colony in the report. So far as I am aware, we are not in any way preparing to make ready use of the available horse resources of the colonies on an emergency, though we know full well we shall want horses, and that we shall not get them from the Continent. The direction of present progress, therefore, does not appear to me to be encouraging.

As regards Coal. In papers presented to Parliament on naval trials of coal, 1877, I find it reported "that the classes of ships comprising the larger proportion of the vessels on the China station should not in future be replaced by similar vessels; *or that coal giving different results should be supplied to the depôts on the station.*" Now the British coal most readily obtainable on that station and on the South Pacific and Indian Ocean, is Australian. Can anyone say which is the principle of our naval policy—whether coal is to be adapted to the ships for service on these stations, or the ships to the coal? Is Mahomet to go to the mountain, or the mountain to Mahomet? Until that question is fairly and practically answered, it is hard to say—as regards coal—in which direction naval progress lies. If, without regard to the nature of British coal found on certain stations, we despatch vessels and fleets with arrangements not adapted to produce maximum results with any other than home coal, we are not making proper use of our available naval colonial resources, and are endeavouring to carry on the defence of an Empire with resources found only in one small corner of it. The question of boiler and furnace arrangements determines a far wider one, viz. whether we are to drag coals across the world to our fleets, or to draw on British resources close at hand. But that is not all. Are we to suppose that because Australian coal does not give equally good results as Welsh coal—in our present ships—that the question ends there? Is Australia to have no naval future because her coal does not exactly suit the war vessels the mother-country chooses to construct to-day? Act as we may, Australia will grow, flourish, and develop, and if we do not now begin to realize the advantage of *dovetailing* our naval system into her available resources, when are we to begin? Turn to Table V., which shows that since the Crimean war, the export of coal from one colony has risen from 60,000 tons in a year to nearly *one million*. Our children now may live to see the annual export of coal from Australia exceed that from the mother-country. Whose business will it be then to protect that supply in war? Will it be England's or Australia's, or our Empire's? The answer to such a grave question can only be dimly discerned through the mists of present naval progress.

It is to be noted that (as will be seen by Table VI.) not quite three million tons of British coal were exported in 1877 to British ports abroad, while over thirteen million tons went to foreign ports. We have every advantage as regards geographical positions for storing coal afforded by our plantation colonies in the West Indies. It is an important fact that out of some 475,000 tons of British coal exported to that quarter of the world in 1877, but 172,000 tons went to the British, while the rest went to the foreign West Indies. Had war broken out in that year, our enemies would in that district of the world have had greater facilities of coal supply than our vessels. In the matter of coal, and as regards these colonies, our progress tends to throw the balance of naval power from them towards ports that in war will be neutral.

As regards Food. Most officers must, I think, have found that naval, military, and marine pensioners are every day finding it more and more difficult to provide at home for themselves and their families. Their families have, as a rule, been brought up in an atmosphere of order, cleanliness, and discipline, and benefited largely by education at the expense of the State. Take these facts into consideration, together with the waste of food-producing resources, and the manifest desirability of fostering cordial feelings in the colonies towards the British seaman and soldier, and reflect that while we are at our wits' end to provide inducements to serve in the army and navy, the word colonies, as suggesting a means to an end, is never even whispered.* Russia, as an inducement to her seamen to settle at Vladivostock, moves their wives and families free of expense from one side of the world to the other, and can we with our magnificent territories do for our seamen's and soldiers' families —nothing? It is important to remember that even now in the great English continent of Australia wondering English children listen to their mother's description of British soldiers once seen by her there, and that is all the next Australian generation will really know about them.

In conclusion, and as directly bearing on the food question in its wider aspects, I commend to earnest attention the following short extract from the proceedings of "The Lords' Committee" on horses. Referring to the incidental allusion to Canada by

* See Appendix III.

Sir H. Storks—a sort of official right-hand of the War Minister of England—the following question was put to him, and the following answer given. *Question:* " In the event of a war with France or any other great naval power our importation of horses would naturally be interfered with, and that would be a great difficulty, would it not? *Answer: Yes, certainly.*" Now if the importation from Canada of a few thousand horses, will when at war with a great naval power "*naturally be interfered with*," what is to become of the fifteen thirty-thirds of our home population dependent on eighteen different lines for their food?

CHAPTER VI.[*]

DEVELOPED RESOURCES.

Shipping.—Having, in Chapter V. briefly touched upon some of the " raw material " of war possessed by the colonies, we have now to glance at their " developed resources." Shipping demands first consideration, for no matter what may or might be the war-power of outlying portions of the Empire, it can only be applied through and by the aid of ships. Table VIII. gives the number and aggregate tonnage of the vessels belonging to the whole Empire, at the same time distinguishing the total mercantile marine possessed by each class of colonies.

It is to be observed that Canada alone stands *fourth* on the list of the mercantile navies of the world; the United Kingdom being *first*, United States *second*, and Sweden and Norway *third*.

The aggregate tonnage of the mercantile marine of Australasia is about equal to half that of Russia, while the mercantile marine of our plantation colonies is more than double that of Portugal. The total aggregate tonnage belonging to our colonial Empire is by more than half greater than that of France, by about half greater than that of

[*] Delivered before Royal United Service Institute, April 4, 1879.

Germany, and not very far short of being double that under the Italian flag.

TABLE No. VIII.

TABLE SHOWING SHIPPING BELONGING TO BRITISH COLONIES AND POSSESSIONS, 31st December, 1877, and Distribution thereof.

Class.	Group.			Total.	
	Name.	Vessels.	Tonnage.	Vessels.	Tonnage.
Colonies Proper.	Canada	7,568	1,211,451		
	Australasia	2,311	245,464		
	Cape*	57	6,271		
	Total Colonies Proper ..			9,936	1,463,186
Plantation Colonies.	West Indies	1,200	70,662		
	Ceylon	248	16,476		
	Mauritius	99	8,770		
	Total Plantation Colonies ..			1,547	95,908
Military and Trading Settlements.	Europe {Gibraltar, Malta..}	207	26,455		
	Straits Settlements	469	54,585		
	Hong Kong	66	20,934		
	West Africa	96	2,996		
	Falkland Isles ..	7	423		
	Total Military and Trading Settlements			845	105,393
	Total Colonies and Settlements			12,328	1,664,487
	Empire of India			187	69,481
	Total Colonies, Settlements, and India			12,515	1,733,968
	Shipping of United Kingdom			25,733	6,399,869
	Total British Shipping			38,248	8,133,837

* St. Helena included.

NOTE.—Shipping returns have not been received from Melbourne since 1865, nor from twenty-two other ports abroad for 1877. The above Table, therefore, probably understates the actual number of vessels and aggregate tonnage,—vide Annual Statement of Navigation and Shipping of the United Kingdom for the year 1877.—Parliamentary Paper C-1999, 1878.

These are interesting and striking facts, and superficially regarded, they are apt to be construed as indications of immense and immediately available maritime power. Let us briefly examine whether this be a correct conclusion.

It will be observed that the military and trading settlements,' taken together, have only an aggregate of 845 vessels, and as these places are scattered and far apart, and the average tonnage per vessel is only about 125, the war value of this portion of the colonial mercantile marine is practically nothing—except as affording the Empire a series of small training schools, in which, free of public expense, men of various races receive nautical knowledge. That knowledge does not of itself, in these days, make a war seaman, *and in the absence of any arrangement by which our navy can strengthen itself in distant parts of the world,* readily and at once, it is, I think, quite possible that, generally speaking, the colonial mercantile marine may—under present circumstances—be found to offer more temptations to our enemies than resources of strength to ourselves.

The plantation colonies only possess one steamer over 800 tons, this belongs to Hong Kong. It appears to me therefore that any resource offered by the mercantile marine of plantation colonies must have reference to men, not ships, and in the absence of any effort on our part to husband and organize such resources, the growth of the plantation mercantile marine increases proportionally the burden on the Royal Navy without adding to its power.

Turning to the colonies proper, Canada owns 9 steamers over 800 tons :—

```
3 over  800 and under 1000 tons.
4   „  1200    „    1500  „
1   „  1500    „    2000  „
1   „  2000    „    3000  „
―
9
```

Australasia has but 3 steamers over 800 but under 1000 tons; it is therefore useless to preach naval "self-reliance and self-defence" to those colonies.

I trust I have said enough to show how necessary it is to look below the surface of figures in the matter of estimating colonial resources of war. I grant that the mercantile marine of a country represents proportionately maritime power, but it is too often forgotten that it is *power in a latent and dormant state.* Its real, actual, available value as a war resource, entirely and altogether depends upon the readiness with which it can be converted from latent power into visible force. Without Imperial arrangements by which such change in the colonial mercantile marine can be readily made, I verily believe there is serious ground for thinking that in the outbreak of war, it may prove a source of naval weakness rather than a source of naval strength. Take Canada, for instance, with a mercantile marine greater than that possessed by any European power, except Sweden and Norway; what a picture is here presented of immense dormant naval power, combined with actual naval helplessness! Our Imperial arrangements are such that though home ports are always more or less filled with effective reserve ships, none are ever laid up in colonial ports. If war broke out, many of these ships kept at home would be commissioned and dispatched to those water districts of which Canada and Australia are the natural bases; but we prefer to bring these ships backwards and forwards across the world at great expense, rather than leave them in reserve in colonial ports, where they could be maintained at perhaps a less cost, and where they would, at all events, be invaluable in peace as naval depôt-centre training ships and schools of instruction for an Imperial naval reserve; while in war they would be more ready to hand for distant service than if laid up in home ports.

If the latent maritime power of the enormous mercantile marine of the colonies is incapable of ready conversion into visible force, and furnishes no practical resource whatever for what we term the Imperial fleet, it is simply because we do not choose to provide the machinery, nor to make the reciprocal arrangements necessary to turn it to account. Meantime the colonies are " growing while we are sleeping," and every year of such growth adds to the defensive duties and responsibilities of the

Royal Navy, without adding to its ability to meet the increased demand. It will be advantageous to defer further remark on this particular portion of the subject, until some general considerations respecting the organization and armed strength of the colonies have been roughly indicated, and to these we will now pass.

REMARKS ON ARMED STRENGTH.

Before attempting to outline the salient features of colonial naval and military organization, &c., it is necessary to define broadly what are the lines of inquiry I propose to adopt. Briefly, then, I may say it appears to me more useful to examine them with a view to forming general conclusions of Imperial importance, rather than attempt to inquire into the merits or demerits of purely local systems, which would be not of general interest, and impossible to do fairly in a short space.

These organizations can only properly be understood by reference to their common origin; the soils, so to speak, in which they have been propagated, and in which some apparently flourish, some languish, and some have withered and died. To trace their common origin to its true source would necessitate examination of questions neither naval nor military, and must not here be attempted; but in order to approach the subject in an intelligible manner, it is necessary to bear in mind the changes in military distribution and organization which have taken place, and also the development of our colonies during a period of remarkable progress and prosperity. To those, therefore, it is necessary in the first place briefly to refer. I leave out entirely Mediterranean stations and garrisons, and, of course, India.

When Her Majesty began to reign, the colonial Empire consisted of 24 colonies and settlements, having in the aggregate less than 4 millions of population, a total revenue of less than $2\frac{1}{2}$ millions sterling, and the total aggregate annual value of their exports and imports was some 30 millions sterling only. At that time we maintained in those colonies a military force of about 27,000, some 10,000 of which were stationed in the West Indies, some 5000 in British North America, then consisting of seven separate colonies; the remainder being quartered at the Cape, in Australasia, Ceylon, Mauritius, and a few other places; the cost of such forces being given in a parliamentary paper at some $1\frac{1}{2}$ million sterling. The Crimean war found the foregoing distribution but little changed in principle, though some variations in detail had taken place. For example, the West Indian garrison had fallen from 10,000 to about 5000, while the Australian had risen to a total of 4000. A parliamentary paper published in 1859 shows the average Imperial force maintained in these colonies in each year, from 1853 to 1857 inclusive, to have been nearly 27,000. I again remind you I exclude Mediterranean stations. This force included six resident corps,* borne on the strength of the Royal army, and provided for in the army estimates, all of which have since been abolished. In 1858, just twenty years after the date here taken as the starting-point of comparison, there still was no change in *principle* of distribution, nor much variation in the cost of maintenance, but the following remarkable changes had taken place meantime in the position of the colonies; the aggregate population had more than doubled, the revenue had more than quadrupled, the annual value of their exports and imports had trebled,† and the number of colonies had increased by eight.

The principle of military distribution, however, though it had stood a test of many years and two great national struggles, one in the Crimea and one in India, was open to one great military objection, viz. that the disposable force being limited and inelastic, the permanent quartering abroad of so large a proportion, left the garrison of the grand base, the United Kingdom, dangerously weak. The militia had been neglected, no reserve had been provided, and in spite of the repeated warnings of the most eminent military

---

* Newfoundland Companies, Ceylon Rifle Regiment, Cape Mounted Rifles, St. Helena Regiment, Gold Coast Artillery Corps, and Falkland Island Company.

† 1858. Aggregate of colonial population, 8,148,641; revenue, 10,259,292*l.*; value of exports and imports of the colonies, 93,630,750*l.*

authorities, no system whatever had been provided for the defence of these Islands, nor for strengthening and supporting the army quartered at home, except by calling in the outlying portion.

There was one other objection, which on purely military grounds had good foundation. All the colonial positions occupied by Imperial troops had not been chosen for Imperial naval or military reasons, nor were the numbers regulated so much with regard to military necessities as by trade interests and political causes. The very best strategic positions we had taken by force, and knew their worth, having learned it by the bitter experiences of great naval wars. Since those wars, great developments had taken place, the foundations of branch British nations had been laid, and a new world of civilization and progress opened in the Pacific. The simple fact that we have not yet had to fight for strategic positions in the South Pacific, may in some way account for the circumstance that we never did and do not now maintain any Imperial naval establishment there. The original causes of our having troops in Australasia were not military, but purely civil, and we find them there in 1858, long years after the civil necessities for the presence of military force had ceased.

This, then, was the state of things twenty years ago, and it is quite plain that the theory of English defence then, as handed down to us by naval experience, was based on the assumption of necessity for being prepared for an attack at any part of our position, and that the arrangements for the defence of an Empire could not be confined to but one portion of it only. In practice it was defective, because, as before remarked, many of the positions were not well chosen; and political and trading interests had overruled military caution and thus left the United Kingdom so weak as to be well-nigh defenceless. Up to the time to which I refer, the military forces of the Empire consisted of regular troops and militia. The constitutional machinery by which the State could organize and train English manhood into an armed militia for purposes of defence existed. It was rusty and required oiling and repairing, but nevertheless the power existed and was ready to hand at home and in the colonies. Military authorities had for years been endeavouring to have it examined, repaired, and improved, but successive Governments paid no heed to their warnings, for the nation looked upon such matters with coldness and apathy. Then suddenly came the invasion panic, arising from the unexpected declaration of war by France against Austria and the rapidity of its consequence. This panic was really due to an acknowledgment of the powerlessness of resisting direct attack upon the Imperial base which military opinion had been for years persistently, but vainly, pointing out to a nation that would not see. Before anyone had time to think, an enormous section of the English people of Great Britain had rushed to arms and was busy organizing and drilling itself into a volunteer army. Government *followed* whither the movement led. The militia were for a time forgotten, and the theory of voluntary local or home defence was established as a cardinal principle of our military system, and rapidly took such deep root in the English mind at home as to gradually produce a complete revolution of our colonial military arrangements. It soon became apparent that the invasion question was not so simple as uneducated popular military enthusiasm imagined. Attention consequently turned to the militia and to the army. This at once involved serious financial considerations, and thus military expenditure in the colonies became a part of the question of the defence of the English coast-line, while the defence of the colonies ceased to be a national military question and came to be regarded as something not of Imperial concern, but of local and individual interest to each colony only. Having sprung from a common origin it is not therefore surprising to find that all colonial defensive systems have leading characteristics in common, distinctly traceable to the mode and circumstances under which the creation of such systems became, more or less suddenly, necessary. It is, however, right to say that the particular history and circumstances of each colony largely influenced the nature and degree of the individual efforts made. For example, Canada at once started with a militia system of a business-like character to which I shall presently refer, while other colonies mainly relied upon the voluntary efforts of patriotic individuals to whom permission was given to organize defences subject to certain conditions. On the one hand, Government assumed the responsibility of compelling citizens to defend their country: on the other, Government, in many instances, avoided the responsibility by leaving it to the citizens to do so or not as they liked. But however different at starting may have been the mode of proceeding by which military safety was intended to be attained, there was one fundamental principle lying at the root of all. It was this—that the defence of each colony concerns itself only and should therefore be of a purely local character: in a word, that the "open sesame" of colonial safety lies in the two words—Home Defence. That term is now popular throughout our Empire, but the general adoption of the military principle involved is, I think, worthy of serious critical examination. I have often asked, What are the territorial limits as defined by the word "Home" in conjunction with the word "Defence"? I have never seen a reply. But it may be useful to point out that in Great Britain the obligation of Home Defence is deemed to end—for the greater portion of our military forces—at the water's edge: while in Australian colonies it has been assumed to terminate at a land line marked on the map as separating two English colonies: and I could name a colony elsewhere which, by a carefully and elaborately drawn law, declared it to end at the precise distance of four miles from the capital! No officer or man was to be compelled even to march beyond that magic line, and could not even be called out within it until the enemy practically was in sight. So far was this principle of local obligation carried at the Cape, that up to last year the military organization for the defence of the colony was by territorial divisions, the inhabitants being "organized for the internal defence," *not* of the colony, but merely of "their respective divisions." When trouble came, its chief sting lay in the fact that military combinations had been legally paralyzed by Act of Parliament. In New Zealand, at this moment, "no militia officer or militiaman in any regiment can be carried or ordered to go beyond the boundaries of the districts for which such regiment or independent company is raised, except only such as shall volunteer for service out of the same." *

No one will dispute there are greater facilities for safe and rapid intercommunication between all parts of the British Empire now, than there were between all parts of England in the thirteenth century. It is an interesting fact that in 1285 the English freeman armed for defence was not protected by law from leaving his county or shire "upon the coming of strange enemies into the

* *Vide* 'New Zealand Militia Act, 1870.'

realm."* The truth is, the British Empire in its military constitution now is not so far advanced as England 600 years ago.

Now it may be said we have regular troops enough to move to every part of the Empire when wanted, and therefore it is not in a naval and military sense objectionable for each part of the Empire to tie up its forces with parliamentary strings. But when the Empire is acting on its defence, its small regular army, being its only English arm of attack, must not be absorbed by even Imperial positions of passive defence abroad; and if all the rest of the military forces are immovable, our Imperial position cannot be made strong at the points where it should be strongest. When we recollect that in order to send a handful of troops to Zululand we had almost to break up several regiments, we should not be too sure that our only movable force is prepared to stand an Imperial strain. But it may be said these local military forces, home and colonial, are merely supplementary. If so, let it be clearly understood to what they are supplementary. At home no doubt they are supplementary to the regular army, their duties and positions being clearly defined; but what do colonial forces supplement? Not a general plan of Imperial defence, for no such plan or scheme exists. The principle on which we rely for ensuring a mamxium amount of Imperial safety, with a minimum of force and

* 'Military Forces of the Crown,' Clode.

expenditure, is in itself vague. It is shortly expressed in the concluding paragraph of the report of the Select Committee of the House of Commons in 1861. "Your Committee submit that the tendency of modern warfare is to strike blows at the heart of a hostile power; and that it is therefore desirable to concentrate the troops required for the defence of the United Kingdom as much as possible, and to trust mainly to naval supremacy for securing against foreign aggression the distant dependencies of the Empire." From this it would appear that colonial military forces are supplementary to naval supremacy, or rather that it is reasonable to regard them as supplementary to our fleets. Now the power of a fleet is in proportion to its absolute freedom from duties of territorial defence. The two leading principles of naval distribution may be said to be—1st, Off the enemy's coast; 2nd, Covering the commanding points of communications on the high sea. To secure our naval bases and to furnish sufficient means for their local defence is an Imperial duty which I humbly submit we ought no longer to shirk, and in its discharge should seek to enlist the hearty co-operation of our brother Englishmen in the colonies. It is to be observed that if military forces, created as supplementary to naval power, are constituted on the principle of *immobility*, the operations of the fleet become dependent on the regulation of military forces rather than on the necessities of the naval work to be done. The naval bases must be then selected, not because they are most suitably situated, but because military forces have established themselves regardless of naval necessities. There is no alternative between that and a sacrifice of naval power by using sea-going force to protect fixed points. But there is one more danger arising from the adoption of the principle of immobility of military force to which I desire to draw attention. If fragmentary local protection be a sound military principle of Imperial defence, but a short step leads to localizing naval defence, either by Acts of Parliament, or still more surely, by war vessels incapable of keeping the sea. Already there are distinct proofs of naval colonial defence—to say nothing of home—theories developing local proclivities. I observe so eminent an authority as Sir W. Jervois recommending, for example, South Australia to expend some 150,000*l*. of her capital and 13,000*l*. a year of her revenue on a three-masted ironclad for purposes of local defence. She is not to be a regular sea-going ship, but is to be fit to go a certain distance, equivalent to that between Lisbon and the Azores. Sir W. Jervois thus officially speaks of the duties of the Royal Navy in Australian waters: "The Imperial squadron, small, and composed of wooden vessels, being charged with visiting the islands of the South Sea, with the defence of the Fiji Islands, New Zealand, and all Australian colonies; the chance is but small of its being available for the special defence of any one colony or any particular portion of the coast."* We have here a clear illustration of the Imperial programme for maintaining economically our naval supremacy. We annex Fiji, being a position of great strategic importance, a necessary point at which to store coal and naval supplies, and as soon as we have got it, it simply becomes a burden to our fleet, because we do not choose to prepare to locally protect it, and because the military forces supplementary to our fleets are immovable, and none can be detached to so important a position. We took the point as a means of strengthening our naval position, and our arrangements are such that we must weaken our naval position to defend the point. I have thus dwelt at some length on the one principle, common to all our colonial defence systems, because it appears to me to deserve very serious consideration. I venture to think it may lead us by a perilous path to an Imperial slough of naval and military weakness.

As regards the influence of local circumstances on the nature and growth of colonial systems springing from a common original cause, I submit but one brief general observation. It would be unreasonable to expect all colonies to have acted alike when no sealed pattern, as it were, was left as a guide, and no steps taken to assist in securing uniformity. Canada had, and has still, exceptional

* *Vide* 'Sessional Papers, South Australia,' 1877.

advantages, not only enabling her, but prompting her to strike out a military policy more or less distinct. She has, what other great colonies have not, a great and glorious military history of her own. Before she was called upon to organize her military system, she had organized a considerable militia force; and further, large bodies of the regular army, of all branches, had for generations been quartered in her cities and towns. Besides all this, she is an old-settled country, and having passed the feverish time of petty provincial jealousies, seeks, as a united Dominion, a system worthy of consolidated power and enlarged responsibility. It is but right to make this observation, for much misapprehension prevails at home as to the varied circumstances and conditions of other colonies as regards military capability and power, and some colonies are often ignorantly blamed for what they cannot help.

I will now briefly indicate outlines of military organization in the colonies.

ARMED FORCE.

Canada. The militia consists of all male inhabitants between the ages of 18 and 60. It is divided into four classes.

> 1st Class. Men from 18 to 30 years, who are unmarried or widowers without children.
>
> 2nd Class. Men from 30 to 45, who are married or widowers with children.

3rd Class. Men from 45 to 60.

The above is the order in which the male population is called upon to serve.

The Militia is divided into Active and Reserve.

The Active Militia consists of the Volunteer Militia, the Regular Militia, and the Marine Militia: the Volunteer Militia being composed of corps raised by voluntary enlistment; the Regular Militia, of men who have voluntarily enlisted to serve in the same, or who have been balloted to serve; the Marine Militia composed of seamen, and persons whose usual occupation is upon any steam or sailing craft. The Reserve Militia consists of the whole of the men who are not serving in the Active Militia for the time being. The period of service, in time of peace, in the Volunteer Militia is three years, in the Regular and Marine Militia two years. Men enrolled in the service companies of Regular or Marine Militia during any such two years are not again liable to be taken for drill and training until all the other men in 1st, 2nd, or 3rd Class of the same " company division " have volunteered or been balloted to serve. No member of a Volunteer Militia corps can, in time of peace, resign under six months' notice.

Canada is divided into twelve Military Districts; these are subdivided into Brigade and Regimental Divisions, and again into Company Divisions.

In each Regimental Division, one lieutenant-colonel and two majors of Reserve Militia are appointed from the residents therein; all Militia orders and reports are sent to and received through them. In each Company Division one captain, and one lieutenant, and one ensign are likewise appointed to the Reserve Militia. These are responsible by seniority to the regimental staff. Enrolment is carried on by officers of Company Divisions, and the list is corrected before 28th February every fifth year; from the company returns the regimental rolls are made up. "The enrolment," for which the company officers are responsible, is " held to be an embodiment of all the militiamen enrolled, and renders them liable to serve, unless exempt by law." *

The following, though enrolled, are exempted from active service, except in case of war, invasion, or insurrection : Half-pay officers of Her Majesty's army and navy, seafaring men, and sailors actually employed in their calling, pilots and apprentice pilots during the season of navigation, masters of public and common schools.

Her Majesty is empowered by the Act to make such regulations for the enrolment of such horses as may be necessary for the purpose of field artillery and cavalry.

* Exemptions: Judges, clergy, ministers of religion, professors in colleges and universities, or teachers of religious orders, warden keepers, guards of penitentiaries, officers, keepers, and guards of public lunatic asylums, persons disabled by bodily infirmity, and " the only son of a widow being her only support."

The oath to be taken by all ranks of Active Militia is simply as follows: "I, *A. B.*, do sincerely promise and swear that I will be faithful and bear true allegiance to Her Majesty." It can be administered by the commanding officer.

When the Active Militia is to be organized for drill or actual service, and enough men do not volunteer in any company division to complete the quota required from that division, the men in the 1st class are balloted first; if the number of men required is greater than the whole number in 1st class, then the 2nd class is required to make up the deficiency, and so on through each class; but at no time, says the Act, " shall more than one son belonging to the same family, residing in the same house—if there be more than one inscribed on the militia roll — be drawn, unless the number of names so inscribed be insufficient to complete the required proportion of service men."

Appointments of officers to the Active Militia are provisional, pending the taking out of a certificate of fitness from one of the military schools of the Dominion.

According to the Act, officers of Her Majesty's regular army are always reckoned senior to militia officers of the same rank, whatever be the dates of their respective commissions.

The present law permits the training annually of a number not exceeding 45,000 all ranks. The training period for Active Militia, called out for training, is not to exceed sixteen, nor to be less than eight days in any one year.

Non-commissioned officers and privates of mounted corps receive, for each day's drill of three hours, 75 cents for each horse that has taken part in the drill; and every officer and man of the Regular and Marine Militia, and the officers of Reserve Militia, called out for training, receive 50 cents for each day's drill. Payment for drill is made on proof of compliance with regulations touching the drill and efficiency of the several corps.

The militia, or any part of it, may be called out for "actual service," either within or without the Dominion, whenever it appears advisable to do so by reason of war, invasion, or insurrection, or danger of any of them, and when so called out, it may be placed by Her Majesty under the orders of the commander of Her Majesty's regular forces in Canada, and will be paid at such rates of daily pay as are paid in Her Majesty's service.

Officers and men, when called out for actual service, and also during the period of annual training, or during drill or parade of their corps, or as spectators, or while wearing uniform, are subject to the rules and articles of war, and Mutiny Act, the Queen's regulations and orders for the army, and all other laws applicable to Her Majesty's troops in Canada, and not inconsistent with the Canadian Act.

Such are, I believe, the chief characteristics of the framework on which Canada has raised her military organization. I beg it to be remembered that my sketch is a very crude and rough one, and quite unworthy of a subject which should be treated in a separate lecture, and demands, not only more detailed knowledge than I possess, but also a personal experience of its working, which is an honour I cannot claim.

The Reserve Militia numbers some 655,000; it is duly regimentalized, and in some measure efficient, but has not been mustered since 1873. The strength of the Active Militia is in round numbers some 43,700 all ranks.

Field Artillery—18 Batteries	1,326
Garrison	3,048
Engineers	232
Cavalry	1,803
Infantry	37,320
	43,729

There is a Royal Military College at Kingston, one School of Gunnery, called A battery, also at Kingston; and another, B battery, at Quebec. There are besides numerous rifle associations, and a Dominion Artillery Association. I venture to commend to very serious attention the prize essays of the latter Association (one of which will be found in the 'Journal'*). I do so, not only on account of their great value as a contribution to military

* No. 94, p. 184 *et seq.*

literature, but as giving some idea of the progress that association and the schools of gunnery have made and are making under the able auspices of Colonels Strange and Irwin, R.A.

There is a Minister of Militia and Defence charged with and responsible for the administration of militia affairs, including all matters involving expenditure. The Canadian Parliament votes, of course, the application for Militia and Defence annually according to its judgment.

I shall briefly refer again to Canada in summing up my remarks, but before passing to other colonies, it is but right to recall the fact of offers of Imperial service which in 1877-78 came across the sea from the Great Dominion. "These offers," says the official report,* "some of personal service, others to raise battalions, bore the stamp of a thorough determination to give willing and material reinforcements to Her Majesty's troops. They were the spontaneous expressions of a loyal and a high-spirited people to throw in their lot as a very important factor in the destinies of Great Britain. These offers were as cordially received by the Imperial Government as they were loyally made, and should the occasion have arisen, no doubt but that the hardy and stalwart sons of Canada would have been found standing manfully shoulder to shoulder with their native-born brethren of that 'old country' which they love so well.

* *Vide* 'Report on State of Militia, Canada, 1877.'

"But withal, it would have been a question for careful thought, to determine to what extent such a contingent should have been accepted. It would be unwise and perhaps dangerous to denude this country too largely of its fighting men."

Newfoundland.—In Newfoundland—occupying so important an Imperial position geographically, both with respect to Canada and to England—what do we find in the way of defence? Nothing whatever; not even a militia law in force. Several volunteer companies were established some years since, with an enlistment of three years, on the expiring of which term they were broken up. We handed over to this colony some nine forts and batteries, such as they were, an ordnance yard, wharf, and engineer workshops. From 1870 to 1877, not one halfpenny has been spent under the head of military disbursements by Newfoundland. Here, then, is a specimen of the results of trusting the defence of our Empire to a voluntary principle of "home defence." Remember that Newfoundland is a sort of uvula in the Great St. Lawrence throat through which the Dominion breathes; and weigh this fact, that it is not a part of her military system even, and she may suffer by the neglect and inability of the inhabitants of Newfoundland.

Australian Group.—In Australia there are seven different colonies, and therefore it would be utterly impossible here to describe separately each system of military organization and progress, the more especially as none of these several systems have been exactly constant qualities, many have been spasmodic, and others exceedingly variable.

Canada in 1868 founded her military system on a carefully drawn, carefully considered "Militia and Defence Act," of which I have indicated the leading principles. That Act has not been altered. The Dominion Government at once took the responsibility of providing for its military necessities, and of adopting principles of organization which were obligatory on all its citizens. Australian colonies did the reverse. They avoided the responsibility by authorizing such inhabitants as were moved by a military spirit to organize defence. It is a remarkable fact, and one of curious interest, that when Englishmen, at home, rushed to arms and formed themselves into Volunteer Corps—in 1859—they were only doing what Englishmen in the colonies had done in 1854. When the Imperial Parliament reorganized and incorporated Volunteer Corps as a part of the defence system of Great Britain, it was only following in the footsteps trodden years before by Colonial Parliaments in the South Pacific.

Now, while Canada has been steadily developing her system, Australian colonies have been perpetually altering theirs. There are, on the parliamentary records of these colonies, an aggregate of nearly fifty Acts of a military and naval nature, one colony alone having passed twenty Statutes to enable inhabitants to provide for their safety. Now this is our fault, I think, not theirs, and therefore I do not mention the circumstance for the purpose of disparaging their gallant though spasmodic military experiments, which, while costing them very considerable sums of money, have in some cases produced no adequate result, and in others absolute waste. At this moment it is impossible to say—as regards *every* Australian colony —what is the precise strength and nature of existing organizations, or what are the Australians' bills for defence for 1877-78. It is, however, desirable to give an outline of the military system, &c., of each colony roughly and briefly. I must premise that the facts I am about to lay before you, so far as they relate to the actual forces existing in Australian colonies, except West Australia and New Zealand, I extract from an official memorandum of June, 1878, by Lieutenant-Colonel Scratchly, R.E., now officially employed out there, not, however, by the Imperial Government, but by the Australian colonies.

New South Wales.—" In New South Wales the local forces are composed of—1. A Permanent Force, raised somewhat upon the old English army system, the defects of which are perpetuated without any corresponding advantages. Although the force is almost everything that can be desired for fighting purposes, it possesses defects of organization that must in the end prove fatal to the maintenance of a permanent force in these colonies on a satisfactory footing. 2. A Naval Brigade, governed by special regulations under the Volunteer Act, and intended for service afloat. 3. A Volunteer Force, enrolled on the principle of granting land orders for efficient service, a system which has been found not to give the desired result; consequently, without altering the Act, a revision of the regulations for the government of the force has been proposed by Colonel Richardson, the Commandant, in accordance with Sir W. Jervois' recommendation. Under these regulations continuous training for a few days during each year, besides a certain number of drills in daylight, are rendered compulsory in return for a money payment. This reform will constitute a valuable experiment, from which the other colonies should profit.

"In Queensland there is only a Volunteer force, and the maintenance of a permanent nucleus has not yet been decided on. A Bill is now before the Legislature of the colony, which embodies the suggestions made by Sir W. Jervois.

"The Tasmanian and South Australian permanent forces are about to be raised, and Volunteer forces are being enrolled; but the question of organization is under consideration. In South Australia the money-payment system is likely to be adopted.

"In Victoria the local forces comprise—1. A Permanent Force. 2. A Naval Reserve, governed by special regulations, but enrolled under the same Discipline Act as the Permanent Artillery. 3. A Volunteer Force, upon the purely voluntary principle. The Land Order system was also tried in Victoria without any good result, and it has been abandoned."

It is to be observed that no allusion is made by Colonel Scratchly to West Australia or New Zealand. The latter colony declined* to have the advice of Sir W. Jervois and Colonel Scratchly,

---

* With reference to this statement, to the effect that New Zealand "declined to have the advice of Sir W. Jervois, on the ground that it had no money to spend on precautions for external defence," it is desirable to say that the assertion was based on New Zealand Parliamentary Paper, A 6—1877, in which Government stated, "They might, with little warning, have to make provision for resisting an 'internal enemy,'" and that "the state of the finances of the colony at present is such, that it is their duty to avoid expenditure on public works for the defence of the many harbours of the colony."

Sir Julius Vogel (Agent-General) has, however, kindly drawn my attention to the erroneous impression my words may convey, and informs me that:—

"The Government had a report from Sir W. Jervois, which that distinguished Officer prepared in 1871, showing the defences required for the principal ports of New Zealand. Therefore the Government did not consider it necessary to ask Sir W. Jervois and Colonel Scratchly to visit the colony. The report referred to was sufficient to enable the Imperial Government to make specific recommendations to the Colonial Government. The latter at once accepted it, and undertook the entire cost; and the armaments, &c., for the purpose, are now on their way to New Zealand."

It is satisfactory to learn that the valuable services of Colonel Scratchly, R.E., have, since Sir Julius Vogel's correction, been engaged by this colony, and though this officer is not the recognized head of the Australasian British forces, he is practically the one adviser in military matters of every Australasian colony except Fiji.

on the ground that it had no money to spend on precautions for external defences, and West Australia is too poor to provide any such means single-handed. New Zealand has Militia and Volunteer laws in force, every man between the ages of seventeen and fifty-five being compulsorily enrolled in the Militia, but actual service is limited by the bounds of Militia districts, and I believe I am correct in stating that the Militia of New Zealand only exists on paper. In West Australia there is a Volunteer force.

The total armed strength of all these colonies is shown in Table IX. I regret that space forbids my entering into an examination of the cost of these local isolated efforts of each colony without a nucleus of regular interchangeable forces. My calculations lead me to conclude that they are most expensive, and that the United Kingdom and each of the colonies are wasting money for want of common-sense business-like co-operation.

Let me, however, give you one instance, in order to impress you, at all events, with the feeling that there is good ground for serious inquiry. Tasmania is, in a general sense, a position of very great importance to the Empire in Australian waters. Between 1860 and 1871 inclusive, that colony spent over 18,000*l.* on works, arms, and ammunition, and 27,000*l.* on maintenance of Volunteers. That force " melted in air, thin air," and from 1872 to 1875 no military ex-

TABLE No. IX.

STATEMENT OF BRITISH LOCAL ARMED STRENGTH (*all Ranks*) OF AUSTRALASIA.

Colony.	Permanent Forces.		Volunteer Forces.		Volunteer Signal and Torpedo Corps.	Total.	Remarks.
	Naval.	Military.	Naval.	Military.			
New South Wales	..	358	286	2,648	46	3,338	Exclusive of Public School Corps of 1157.
Victoria	119	195	229	3,060	30	4,533	This Corps has only just been re-organized. There were no Officers in 1877.
South Australia ..	..	..	..	725	..	725	
West Australia ..	..	..	..	361	..	361	
Tasmania	..	..	Reorganizing.			..	
New Zealand ..	..	..	431	4,004	..	4,435	Exclusive of Cadet Corps of 1710.
Queensland	..	..	..	1,094	..	1,094	Exclusive of Cadet Corps of 150.
Total	119	553	946	12,792	76	14,486	

penditure consequently was incurred. Parliament inquiry in 1875 brought out the fact that the Volunteer force consisted of but twenty-eight all told, and that it had not been drilled nor inspected since 1871. The 27,000*l.* might just as well have been thrown into the sea. Now, respecting the 18,000*l.* spent in addition on works, arms, and ammunition, I simply give you an extract from an official telegram sent from the Governor, 21st May, 1877, to the Minister for the Colonies in London. After naming guns and ammunition required, the telegram concludes thus: " I earnestly beg help for poor colony: strategically important: making efforts, what you cannot give agents pay."

I have watched the military history of Tasmania in common with other colonies, and for fear of being misunderstood, I wish to say I do not mean to imply that that waste of money was anyone's fault in particular, but is the natural result of a vicious system, or rather of the absence of any Imperial system at all. During the " war scares " of 1877–78, while Englishmen at home were talking of going to Constantinople, Englishmen abroad were thinking of their lives and properties, *and of their sea trade lines*; and these cannot be injured without the Empire being seriously hurt. Besides being bound together by nationality, loyalty, and natural sentiment, we are closely knit by self-interest and trade connection; but in matters of defence, we seem to prefer to trust to fickle fortune rather than to business-like co-operation and common-sense precautions.

The Cape.—This colony at present furnishes ample fuel for a burning question, and well it nay; but the subject under consideration does not admit of our turning aside to give it special or exceptional examination. I would, however, remark, that it is the only colony proper in which are quartered regular troops for internal defence, and that the hour is close at hand when the whole question of Colonial and Imperial responsibility as regards *internal* order and *defence* will be raised for the last time perhaps in the history of the Empire. The opening of this question will probably afford the very last favourable opportunity for calmly and deliberately considering the reciprocal naval and military duties of England and the colonies in matters of common defence. It is most earnestly to be hoped that this fact will not be forgotten, and that in seeking in peace finality as regards internal colonial defence, we shall not leave the far wider question of Imperial defence to settle itself, or to be settled for us, in the accidents and chances of a great war.

The history of the organization of local forces at the Cape is so simple and instructive that it may be useful to give its brief outlines down to last year. To carry inquiry or remark further would answer no useful purpose, as exceptional causes have, too late, produced exceptional military results.

"In 1855, it was deemed 'expedient to make provision' for enrolling and organizing the able-bodied inhabitants of the colony for the protection of life and property," not, however, within the colony, but "*within their respective districts.*"

This is roughly the preamble of the Act of that year, the salient features of which are as follows :—

1. The enrolment by districts of all male residents therein, between the ages of 20 and 50, save and except certain officials.
2. When necessary for the defence of any divisions of the colony, the Governor was empowered to call out this burgher force for service within the said divisions and not elsewhere, except with the burgher's own consent.
3. The officers to be elected by the force so enrolled.

No provision was made to render the force efficient as a military body; some idea of the discipline may be gathered from the fact that absence when called out, wilful disobedience of orders, were punishable by fine *not exceeding 3l.*, which was the highest penalty, and was only recoverable by civil process. One year later another Act was passed, by which the inhabitants were authorized to form themselves into Volunteer Corps for the defence of their respective divisions; while it exempted such volunteers from serving in the burgher force, it made no other provision for drill, training, or discipline. With such a system the Cape drifted for over twenty years to a natural destiny of trouble. Then came war, to meet which it was created, and in which it at once utterly broke down. This is a picture in miniature of the mode and the manner in which the British Empire is now acting.

I only ask those who are annoyed with their brother Englishmen in South Africa for neglecting to provide efficiently for their defence, to remember that they only did on a very small scale what their own Empire is doing all over the world.

Last year the Acts to which I refer were repealed, and the following Acts were passed:—

1. The Cape Mounted Yeomanry Act.— This provided for a paid corps, not exceeding 3000, to be raised by voluntary enlistment, for general military service within the colony or beyond the border thereof, wherever the interest of the colony may require. Officers to be appointed by the Governor.
2. The Burgher Force and Levies Act, which provided for the enrolment of every male between 18 and 50; it perpetuates the

system of electing officers; it empowers the Governor to call out the force for inspection and rifle practice, as he may direct; and also for actual service. The extreme penalty for absence or for refusing to obey orders when called out is 2*l*., or in default 14 days' imprisonment.

3. The Volunteer Act empowers the Governor to accept services of naval and military volunteer corps, and to make regulations for constitution, pay, and discipline. All forces created under these Acts are liable to service "within the colony or beyond the borders thereof." No annual system of training is provided, nor would any of the corps be under the Mutiny Act, even when on actual service. Now all these Acts have been passed subsequent to the publication of a memorandum by Sir Bartle Frere, containing the following extract:—" I feel assured a militia on the English plan would be found more efficient and less expensive than any other force of the kind which has been recommended by writers or speakers on the subject."* I draw your attention to the fact that Sir Bartle Frere's opinion is not the basis on which the defensive system of the Cape is framed.

* See Memorandum, 26th December, 1877, "Cape Parliament Papers."

Natal.—It may be useful to treat Natal in the same manner as I have done the Cape. In 1854 a Volunteer Ordinance was framed which made it lawful for persons, with the sanction of the Governor, to form themselves into volunteer corps, to elect their own officers, and to make their own rules. Such volunteers to be exempt from being compelled to serve in any militia or military force which might be raised, and no corps could be compelled to serve at a greater distance than 30 miles from its own head-quarters. This Ordinance was repealed next year, and another Act was passed, in its general principle perpetuating the same system.

I will pursue inquiry no further with regard to the Cape and Natal for fear of confusing between the details of defence in one colony and general principles applicable to all.

The total Volunteer strength of the Cape on the 31st December, 1877, was 3343, of Natal 644, all ranks. At the Cape the force was armed with four different pattern rifles.

I am obliged to leave out all reference under this head to plantation colonies and trading settlements. I do so with regret, for the history of spasmodic local efforts and their results would bring to notice some very extraordinary facts, of great importance in the general question.

Before concluding this review of purely military colonial organization there is one most important aspect of the principle on which we are now acting, which must not and cannot be overlooked. No matter what may be the true value of the colonial developed resources as regards numerical military strength, when weighed in the scale of Imperial necessity for united action and a common plan, such strength is absolutely useless unless properly armed and supplied with ammunition and military materials.

When we adopted fragmentary systems of Home Defence and Local self-reliance as the cardinal principles by which our Empire was to be defended, we made no regulations whatever and no provisions whatever for providing for the supply of arms and munitions of war to the colonies.

We left the question to drift, and it is drifting still. The question cannot be shirked nor avoided by saying the colonies must be self-reliant and buy them, for it really covers a very wide field. It not only concerns the distant positions of our Empire, but enters the very core of our supply system at home. As the colonies pay for what they want and they expect to get at once and at all times, what they require, the question is, *are we prepared to supply them when these demands are largest and most urgent, which will also be the hour of our sorest need?* If any such calamity happened as a rupture with America—which I say, God forbid—could the arsenal at Woolwich with the strain then thrown upon it meet in addition the requisitions of the Canadian army, numbering 600,000, and also the demands of Australasian and Plantation Colonies and Military and Trading Settlements, all pouring in at one and the same time?

This is an extreme case, but during the scare of 1877–78, from numerous colonies came constant telegraphic demands for various descriptions of stores, and if they come thick at such a time, they will come by hundreds when war is declared. We have done nothing whatever to prepare for meeting promptly the enormous extra demands on home supplies, caused by the fluctuations and the growth of military forces in the colonies. Now the principle of individual self-reliance on the part of each fragment of the Empire, involves not only choice as to what defensive organization each adopts, but also the exercise of a free and independent judgment in the selection of weapons and stores. Hence it is that it places home arsenals in the position of not knowing from hour to hour what is the precise nature of the stores colonial governments may demand through the diverse channels of departmental communication. Want of uniformity, produced by absence of a common or Imperial system of defence, renders it utterly impossible to regulate supply efficiently and economically. I cannot extend my remarks further on this head, but when they are considered in a business-like practical manner in conjunction with the broad fact that British fleets and military forces all over the world are, by our present system, compelled to rely mainly on home arsenals, I think my humble opinion will not be found far short of the truth. It is briefly this—that the Imperial supply system will utterly break down under the strain of war.

Before turning to naval colonial organization, let me shortly state the exact point at which the most progressive colonies have now arrived. Canada is finding out that a permauent nucleus of military force is a necessity. For further information I refer you to the latest official report on the state of the militia of the Dominion. Victoria and New South Wales have for some years each had a permanent local military artillery force. Now we abolished local military forces of the Royal Army because experience had proved the principle to be full of defects. Canada seems to be aware of this, for the plan proposed for consideration is to make the small nucleus of three battalions interchangeable with battalions of line in England. It is neither necessary, nor is it now possible, for any colony of Australia to adopt this system on such a scale, because the permanent military forces required to be maintained are small. But if the local forces in Australia are supplementary to naval defence, each nucleus should be adapted to the requirements both of Australian Governments and also to naval power. The practical difficulty of Imperial interchangeability vanishes if the Marine Artillery and Marine Infantry cease to be overlooked. Their organization makes it a matter of indifference whether they have to send a corporal's guard to Botany Bay or thousands to Gallipoli. The Australian Governments must have a guarantee that such nucleus must not be withdrawn in war, and while they bear the cost of their nucleus we must bear the cost of maintaining a corresponding number of their forces at home, treating them in all respects as part and parcel of the Royal Forces, with equal claims as to rank, rewards, and emoluments. The system of the marine artillery makes it a matter of indifference whether its members are called on to instruct naval reserves in gun drill or military forces in all branches—except cavalry and engineering—of military art; and I think inquiry would show this plan, suggested by me many years ago, would be more economical to Australian colonies and not more costly to England than the system now pursued, and would pave the way for that welding together of English war-power of defence into "one harmonious whole," for which we should all earnestly strive.

I conclude this portion of my subject by stating that the aggregate annual revenue of the colonies is now nearly 27,000,000*l*., the aggregate annual value of their exports and imports about 200,000,000*l*. The revenue has therefore increased thirteen-fold, while the annual value of exports and imports is six times what it was when Her Majesty began to reign.

"Naval Armed Strength and Organization."

Under this head I have, as regards Canada, nothing to bring to your notice, except the absence practically of any naval system at all: I desire, however, to draw attention to the fact that—so apathetic are Englishmen now about naval affairs —it has remained for a military officer, Sir Selby Smyth, to urge upon the Canadian Government the adoption of a system of co-operation with the Royal Navy. According to the last Canadian census there are some 16,000 persons whose calling is the mercantile marine; and by Mr. Keefer's excellent handbook it appears there are nearly 53,000 men employed in the fisheries.

Victoria possesses the 'Cerberus,' a harbour-defence ship, and the 'Nelson,' a sea-going wooden vessel. Considerable alterations have been made in this latter vessel within the last year, and, to the credit of the colony be it said, without calling in external aid. The Victorian Act of 1870 provides "that armed vessels maintained by the Colony shall be for the purpose of defending the Coast of Victoria and co-operating, in time of war, with the ships of the Royal Navy, in such manner as the Governor, *with the advice of the Executive Council, shall approve.*"

So far back as 1855, New South Wales passed an Act for maintaining "armed vessels for the service of the colony, for the protection thereof, and for other purposes." Now, with full knowledge of the loyalty and patriotism of Englishmen in the colonies and their liberality as regards expenditure on defence, I cannot think that in the hour of danger, which will also be a time of popular excitement, Executive Councils will be allowed to permit their armed vessels to extend operations beyond the maritime league. Herein lies a source of danger. The Admiralty at home is tolerably certain to regard each colonial armed vessel as a source of British naval strength in Australian seas, and to take credit for it in the estimate of required power, while the Commodore, in those waters, must make his disposition of naval force, which he nominally commands, not in accordance with the necessities forced upon him by the mode of impending attack, but by the views and wishes of different Executive Councils, controlling portions of his fleet. The annual value of exports and imports of Australasian colonies approaches now 100 millions; of this, over 40 millions passes and repasses to the United Kingdom, and it is difficult to conceive a more dangerous naval principle than that which we are now fostering and nourishing in the bosom of Australian seas.

The principle of localizing the action of naval force, whether it be by Acts of Colonial Parliaments, by ships that cannot keep the sea, or by immobility of military forces intended to act in the support of our fleets, to my mind contains the germs of creeping naval paralysis, which, if not checked, will prostrate and finally destroy our supremacy of the sea.

The naval force of Victoria consists of permanent "*Cadres*," numbering 119, maintained on board their two ships, and a naval reserve of 229, which receives a retaining fee to hold itself in readiness to complete the complement of the 'Cerberus' and the 'Nelson.' These vessels' complements would be under the Naval Discipline Act when called out for actual service.

In New South Wales there is a Naval Volunteer Brigade, numbering some 286, and in New Zealand there are five Naval Volunteer Corps, with an aggregate strength of 431. The developed naval resources, therefore, of the mercantile marine of the colonial Empire—which is by half greater than that of France—consists of one harbour defence vessel, one wooden vessel, and a handful of volunteers, some of whom are wholly uninstructed and others certainly undisciplined.* According to the census returns, there are more than 10,000 persons in Australasia whose calling is on the sea; the number at the Cape is infinitesimal.

Captain Marshal Smith, Master of the Australian barque 'T. T. Hall,' writing to the 'Nautical

---

* Colonel G. Arbuthnot, M.P., has, since this was written, exposed in the House of Commons, and in subsequent letters on "Imperial Defence," the total failure of the Colonial Naval Defence Act, 1865, and Colonial Dock (Loan) Act, 1865, and has clearly shown the utter want of any system of co-operation between the mother-country and the colonies in naval preparation.

Magazine,' from the other side of the world, says: "It has often surprised the writer that in all the recommendations for defence, a Colonial Naval Reserve has never been proposed until Mr. Brassey's proposition." He calculated "that 2000 Australian seamen might be trained and organized as a reserve for the Royal Navy." Englishmen, however, seem blind to this colonial resource, and deaf to the utterances of a General in Canada and to the pleadings of a Colonial Merchant Captain at the Antipodes.

Conclusion.

Time compels me to refrain from summing up these two papers in a manner worthy of the subject. I cannot conclude, however, without once more entreating the men who have the power, to obtain inquiry into the workings of our present policy of Imperial defence, which has now been in force for a period approaching ten years. I incline to the belief that it is breeding a series of naval and military confusions; but I sincerely hope I may be wrong. Such an inquiry, I venture to think, must take the form of an Imperial Commission on which should sit representatives of the great colonies, selected by them for the purpose. This Commission should have an advising Council of Naval and Military authorities, to inquire into and to fix the principles on which the Empire must act, in order to secure the maximum amount of safety at a minimum cost. It is a past hope that the great colonies will ever now join in a general scheme, in the construction of which they have had no voice, and in the carrying out of which reciprocal duties and obligations of defence are not clearly defined. "Spreading as the Empire is, over every part of the habitable globe, it is," says Mr. Frederick Young,* " of the utmost importance to inquire by what means its permanent union may be most effectually secured." Now I take it that all Englishmen are agreed on that point, and its naval and military bearing is this:—"*It is of the utmost importance to scientifically 'inquire' by what means Imperial safety in war 'may be most effectually' and economically 'guaranteed.'*"

This we have not yet done.

Having launched our Empire on military and naval planks of self-reliance without any union or any bond, we hope it may drift into a haven of safety; and we or those who come after us may find it stranded amidst the breakers of mutual mistrust.

It is said that the question of Imperial Defence is too big to inquire into as a whole. Well, the Empire is getting bigger and bigger every day, and if we fear to face the problem now, what have we to hope for in procrastination and delay?

We stave off the duty of calm, deliberate inquiry by vague phrases respecting our "supremacy of the sea." We surely ought to inquire and clearly define

* "Imperial Federation," by Frederick Young.

by what method and on what broad principles that supremacy is to be maintained.

This we have never yet done.

Since the introduction of steam revolutionized naval warfare, we have had no National Inquiry to seek out and define the grand principles of naval policy which can be implicitly trusted to rule supreme over every branch and part of our national naval system.

Groping amidst the *débris* of microscopic manipulations and elaborate naval details, the nation has vainly hoped to stumble across Imperial naval principles, and it now finds itself hopelessly confused as to what are great naval principles, and what are—however big—mere details. This has produced national weariness and apathy in naval affairs, and it may end in the decadence of national and naval spirit. Even the English mind cannot be interested in what it cannot comprehend; and once national interest in naval affairs passes into a certain stage of deadly dull disregard, we may well look at our Imperial future with dismay. It was a national naval spirit won our Empire in the past, and must be its hope and confidence in days to come. There are signs now that military longings are—in the popular mind—supplanting naval enthusiasm, and therefore I think the time has come for such a full and searching inquiry as shall cause the English race to pause and reflect upon the practical, real necessities of their Imperial position.

If we drift much longer we know not whither, we shall end we know not where.

Between fatal centralization on the one hand, and false localization on the other, stands "the supremacy of the sea" in the chill cold shade of national negligence: we may well look at it in hesitating doubt, as without close examination it is hard to say if it be a reality. It may be no more than a dream of the past; without inquiry we cannot say. We know it was with us in 1805, we know for certain but little else. For aught we know, the flag lowered to half-mast in the Bay of Trafalgar may have meant more than the death of a hero, and apostle. It may have symbolized the decline of the cause for which he fought and the doctrine for which he died.

For all we really know of the future conditions of naval war, "our supremacy of the sea" may be "pigeon-holed" with the papers of the treaty of Paris or buried for ever in the crypt of St. Paul's.

[APPENDIX I.

APPENDIX I.

Extract from the Naval Prize Essay,* Royal United Service Institution, 1878. *By Captain P. H. Colomb, R.N., on "Great Britain's Maritime Power."*

"My conviction is, that in considering our naval power and its development as a whole, we too commonly fall into the error which is sometimes apparent in our military designs. We are too apt in both cases to overlook the differences which exist in the circumstances of nations, and to regard our own empire as liable to the same dangers and amenable to the same military or naval treatment as all others. We thus commit a double mistake; we suppose that all other nationalities present similar naval and military features—which they do not—and we fancy that we ourselves exhibit a correspondence in circumstances, temper, and character, with that which we have imagined to be common to all our neighbours. Amongst the nations we are like one of our countrymen who happens to own a foreign ancestry, and to carry a foreign air unconsciously. Such a man will often aim at the uniformity which he thinks he perceives around him, unaware of the peculiarities which others see in him, and which being fundamentally natural, can never be shaken off. If we look for it we can readily detect, in the spoken and written words of our foreign naval critics, their opinion

* See 'Journal Royal United Service Institution,' vol. xxii., No. 94.

of the singularity of Great Britain's naval position; and sometimes perhaps we may trace a certain covert surprise on their part, whenever our naval policy appears to *follow* that of any other country.

"History and tradition—our excellent friends if treated with intelligent confidence, but our mortal enemies if allowed an unrecognized sway—are in some degree to blame for this national failing. Many of our famous naval wars have been carried on with nations whose circumstances were not very dissimilar to our own. When the Hollanders fought with us, we both strove for the same prize, the acknowledged dominion of the Narrow Seas. The south and east coasts of England were matched against the shores of Holland. The conditions were alike; the field of battle was localized, and close at hand; so that if the Citizen Navy in its latter days imitated the dash of Prince Rupert, and carried the war into our rivers, the Royal Navy of the Second Charles was glad to borrow the fighting formation of the enemy's fleet. Both nations, in short, fought on an equal footing, were liable to the same dangers, and experienced the same chances of success at sea. It was in the nature of things that their naval views should agree, and should produce identical results in policy. In the French wars prior to those of the Revolution and the Empire, the naval circumstances of France and of England did not so greatly differ. Each had a seaboard trade—vast for that epoch—and while each had growing colonial interests in the West and East, neither nation could be starved into submission by a blockade. When the revolutionary war broke out, the relative situations of the two countries had not materially altered. If Canada had passed to England, England had lost the United States, and France still held her magnificent West Indian colony. If French influence in Hindostan was on the wane, Pondicherry was not the unimportant colonial item it has since become; and a very few years previously, the

French had deemed it politic to maintain a fleet, numerically more powerful than our own, in the Eastern Seas. As the war progressed, the fleets, trade, and colonial possessions of Holland, combining with those of France, restored any balance which might have been overthrown by the progress of our Indian Empire. Lastly, to complete the picture; if at a later period of the war, England trembled under the excitement of a threatened blow from the camp at Boulogne, La Vendée, at an earlier time, might easily have become the stepping-stone of England to a new conquest of France.

"Thus the dim recollection of the glories of the past, often disinclines us to take that calm and firm survey of the present, which can alone dictate a policy capable of securing 'a powerful and economic imperial Naval Force.' History is often allowed to sway us in one way, when, did we adopt its real teachings, it would show that that way was a treacherous by-path. For in what degree, let us ask, does the British Empire of to-day resemble, in its naval aspect, that of any other country? And how far, with the world against us in arms, could we now adopt the naval policy of the close of last century, or be put to the shifts and expedients of a still earlier naval epoch? In none of her former naval wars did England begin with any tangible superiority in her favour; still less could she claim a monopoly of power on her side. When she won her higher place at the close of each war, she did it by the stubborn daring of her naval leaders, and by the superior moral and physical strength of her seamen. Her forces at any menaced point, seldom exceeded the nominal power of those of her enemies, and when she beat them, she did it in spite of the facts. If she now adventures into a naval war—even with the world against her—she does so with one absolute and one practical monopoly in her favour. In the marvellous constellation of naval stations with which she has spangled the ocean, Great

Britain possesses an absolute monopoly of resource. She starts in a war with a connected series of *points d'appui*, which are of overwhelming value, and which cannot be rivalled by the rest of the world banded together. Formerly, the propulsive force of ships was common to all nations. Now that force is unequally distributed, and England possesses it in larger quantity, and in better quality, not only than any single nation, but than any moderate group of nations. The coal fields of Wales produce a steaming fuel that has no rival, and in her great colony at the Antipodes, England holds alike the control of steam power there. In her iron, her inventive power, and her restless industry, she possesses advantages which may easily be added to swell the list of her superiorities at starting; but these she has always possessed, and has always used in achieving her naval supremacy, so I do not add them. But in her coal she has far more than the mere superiority which the quantity and quality of her production supply. Her coal mines combine with her naval stations abroad to give that second 'practical' monopoly of which I have spoken. Coal, before it can become a naval force, must find its way into the bowels of the war ship. England alone possesses the appliances for making this transfer in every quarter of the globe. Her enemies must commonly load with coal in neutral ports in short measure, and in haste and fear. England alone stores her war ships everywhere within the security of her own harbours. Steam, which in popular fears 'bridged the Channel,' in truth and in fact placed in our hands the means of barring every ocean highway to all but British ships.

"But if the progress of time has submitted these vast powers to our control, it has not failed to add corresponding weakness and dangers to our Empire. The power which closed the naval schemes of Napoleon at Trafalgar, was the self-sustaining, self-contained, and self-reliant, eighteen millions of people who lived in the British Islands. However truly the last adjective may apply to the thirty-two millions who have succeeded their ancestors, the two first can no longer do so. In 1813, the British people lived on the produce of their soil. In 1875, that people required *side by side with every pound's worth of raw cotton for manufacture, one pound's worth of raw corn or flour for their sustenance.* In considerations such as the foregoing—which might be multiplied if space permitted—we must recognize one of the great changes in the Empire, since the close of the last naval war. That manufactures and commerce have enormously increased is a well understood fact, but this increase has not so much altered as intensified the conditions which were peculiar to Great Britain in earlier days. The state of the food supply, and the increased population dependent on it, are new elements in the problem, which materially alter the general result. The change is also complete in relation to those outlying colonies of whose enormous value as coaling stations I have spoken. In naval war, under the old conditions, a blow aimed at any of our smaller colonies would have been more dangerous to our prestige than vital to our power at sea. The capture or destruction of a coal depôt on British ground might now inflict a wound which would be well-nigh fatal. Deprived of the supply which was absolutely necessary to their value as fighting ships, the British men-of-war in the vicinity must either fly from an inferior force, or yield to it; and the commerce which depended on their protection, must cease to flow.

"What then is the British Empire in its maritime aspect? It is a vast, straggling, nervous, arterial, and venous system, having its heart, lungs and brain in the British Islands, its alimentary bases in the great possessions of India, Australia, and North America, and its ganglia in the Crown colonies. Through this system pulsates the life-blood of the Empire. Main arteries and corresponding veins lead

East through the Mediterranean and the Red Sea to India, China, and Australia; West to America and the West Indies; South to Australia, Southern Africa and America, and to the Pacific. Capillaries the most minute, at the extremities of civilization, gather up the raw produce of the nations, transmit it to the larger channels, which in their turn convey it to the heart. This tremendous organ having extracted all that is necessary for its own sustentation, forces the transmitted produce through the great main channels, and finally through millions of branching filaments to sustain and revivify the nations of the earth to their remotest borders. The life of an Empire so highly organized, must hang by a thread. It is no mollusc from whose inert substance huge masses may be detached at will without much effect upon its vitality. It is a living organism whose parts are all inter-dependent, and highly sensitive in their relations. A stab at the heart may put it to death more suddenly, but perhaps not more surely, than the severing of a remote artery, or the wound of a 'nerve centre.'

"Assuming that this picture of the British Empire, its strength, and its weaknesses, is a true one, it is well to put the statement to some closer examination. Do we in fact frame our naval policy in correspondence with the facts of our Imperial position? or, would the course we pursue equally fit Russia, France, Germany, or America? Are we recognizing to its full extent our practical monopoly of coal supply? Are we guarding these 'nerve centres'—our coaling stations—with a clear notion of the effect of a wound there? Are the conditions I have sketched familiar to the naval mind of England? Do they form the ordinary argument of public writers and speakers on naval policy? To all these questions, I think we must give such answers as will confirm my statement. From the complications of a naval policy which is sadly driven and tossed by the wind of the day, we may occasionally extract a fact, a thought, or a statement, consonant with a general system; but the rule is the other way.

"Take for instance the invasion scares which every now and then set our wits staggering. I hold that it is impossible for any one whose habit is to regard our Naval Empire as a whole, to share in them. Let us take reasonable precautions by all means against invasion, when, as in the days of Napoleon, the political conditions are such as to render invasion the chief aim of our enemies. But if our precautions are such as will make the invasion of the United Kingdom more difficult, but will render its BLOCKADE by sea more easy, or leave any of these main arteries or nerve filaments—any of the chief channels of food supply, or trade—liable to be cut or blocked, can it be said that we are recognizing our Imperial conditions? Take again the harbour-defence cry, which at the cost of more than a million, built the 'Glatton,' 'Hotspur,' 'Cyclops,' 'Hecate,' 'Hydra,' and 'Gorgon'; if it did not go further and share in the designs of the 'Devastation' and her successors. The building of powerful ships which are not fully sea-going—which are more or less incapable of maintaining the ocean communications of the Empire—can only be justified on the assumption that the chief danger to it lies at the mouth of the Thames, the Mersey, or the Clyde; at Plymouth Sound, Spithead, and the Medway. But if our enemies are to career at will across our lines of communication, while we guard their terminations at headquarters, what will be left us to guard? Take again the exceedingly persistent struggle to produce 'cruisers' which shall be perfect sailing vessels, as well as perfect steamers, but necessarily sacrificing coal stowage, steadiness of platform, offensive or defensive power. Is this difficult enterprise embarked in with a clear conviction that these ships can always have a coaling station under their lee, an advantage of which their enemies are deprived? It is manifest that if the full rig of any ship be reduced to an insignificant auxiliary, she may be made by so much the more powerful a fighting ship. Our enemies' 'cruisers' will be forced to carry a sail power which is not necessary to us. When we submit our fighting ships to the inconvenience of full rigs, are we not throwing away one of the advantages of our naval position? Note again, the energetic development of the torpedo in which we are engaged. Setting aside the argument as to the relative value of particular forms of this weapon, is its development by us, subordinated to the conditions under which we shall carry on a naval war? The various forms of towing torpedo, as well as the locomotive weapons, tend to make attack cheap, and therefore to put into the hands of a weak and struggling naval power, the means of dealing effectual blows to a powerful navy. Their chief field of usefulness will be from a blockaded port, against the force blockading it. Are we wisely preparing to take the place of the blockaded instead of that of the blockading force? The fixed torpedo is a purely defensive weapon, whose only use is the defence of the land against a superior naval attack; is that to be the position of our land in any part of the world during the next naval war?"

APPENDIX II.

Extract from a Lecture on " The Strategic Importance of Military Harbours," * by General Collinson, R.E.

I HAVE not herein proposed any new project for the defence of the Empire, but only the completion into a more perfect system of that policy which has been already begun. It may be described generally as effecting the security of Great Britain itself by local means, and the systematic and combined organization of the regular army and navy for defensive action against the enemy.

This will, perhaps, be thought to be a more aggressive policy than that which this country has generally followed. I don't think it is likely that Great Britain will ever be accused of having an aggressive policy; her vitality depends so much on peace, that her greatest enemies must acknowledge that she has nothing to gain by war and much to lose. Hence the best war-policy for her is that which will soonest bring peace—peace without injury.

I maintain that the policy herein advocated is not only the most effective to that end, but is the only one by which Great Britain can expect to be able to terminate a war except to her own loss. The multiplying of sentinels by sea or land round our coasts, the escorting of our own sea-traffic, or the stopping of that of the enemy, will not of themselves bring a war to a conclusion satisfactory to

* See 'Journal Royal United Service Institution,' vol. xviii., No. 77.

Great Britain, because she herself is the only Power that would be vitally affected by a war system of that nature.

But there is the other argument in favour of its adoption by England, that we are the only nation that can use it effectually. Our coal and iron, our adventurous seafaring habits, our insular position, together constitute a special power in the hands of this country, so remarkable at this epoch of our history, that it would almost seem to have arrived at its perfection for the express purpose, and at the express time required for the security of our interests.

I might also advocate as a necessity, on the higher ground of our responsibilities to those nations placed under our protection; but as that argument would lead me altogether beyond my subject, I will content myself with a final reason in its favour of a more homely character, namely, that it would be economical. The combination of our war forces by land and sea into one system, would no doubt lead to our having a War Department in reality as well as in name, and could, therefore, hardly fail to produce economy, not only by direct reduction of certain expenses now required in duplicate, but by the greater efficiency and more determined action of a single controlling power over our war policy. It would realize the idea of one of the wisest soldiers of our day, Sir Henry Harness, R.E., that " The War Minister of England should be strategist of the Empire, and the units he should deal with are Fleets and Armies."

APPENDIX III.

Extract from a Lecture by Lieutenant-Colonel T. B. Strange, R.A. (Commandant Dominion School of Gunnery), on " The Military Aspects of Canada." *

In considering the question of a Canadian contingent for Imperial service, it would be manifestly unjust and impolitic to allow many of the young men of a young country to be absorbed by military service in Europe, without making provision for their final return and settlement in Canada. To the young men themselves and their relatives it would be equally cruel and unjust to pay them off in London or elsewhere, at the conclusion of their service, with a few pounds in their pockets, perhaps to become waifs and strays of the great floating demoralized population of some great city. Undoubtedly emigration is one of the great questions of the day, which will not be answered by "Drift." 40,000,000 on a comparatively small island, with inadequate food supply and failing manufactures; on the other side of a ten days' sail, 4,000,000 scattered along a riband of 4000 miles, i.e. the population of one city, London, occupying or rather struggling with the cultivation and development of a territory as large as Europe, with an arable area equal to that of Europe without Russia.

Manufacturing magnates may for manifest reasons discourage emigration, neglect our colonies, keeping home population at starvation point, until they have been met

* See 'Journal Royal United Service Institution,' vol. xxii., No. 102.

by strikes that paralyse industry, and threaten to transfer our trade to foreign countries; then instead of telling the people to emigrate, they are taught to clamour for those agrarian laws that will sooner or later shake Great Britain, as they shook Rome, to her very foundation, unless the emigration question is systematically considered and encouraged. We have been willing to struggle for black empire as long as it required cotton clothing, but as soon as it threatens to cover its nakedness without Manchester help, we say perish India! or Africa, or anywhere else that won't clothe itself with our cotton, and yet we ignore the manifest means of protecting ourselves by a commercial Zollverein with our colonies. Surely British merchants don't need to be taught by British soldiers that commerce means empire, and *vice versâ*. The German Empire was consolidated by commerce, not cannon. The treaty of Zollverein, in 1831, paved the way for that reunion of the German Principalities consummated at Sedan, yet we seem indifferent to the commercial development of an Anglo-Saxon Empire and its commercial relations with ourselves, which are surely capable of adjustment to the mutual development of ourselves and our colonies. Canada has already led the way by proposing differential duties against the United States, manifestly in favour of Great Britain, whose press, misunderstanding the points at issue, has met her with expressed displeasure, instead of encouragement.

True there is room for uneasiness as to how far the trade self-protection of Australia and Canada, as opposed to protection of the general Imperial interests, may be carried, but the game is yet in our own hands. Commercial union with our colonies is surely possible, unless we decline to discuss the matter with them, and prefer the system of "drift." Let us remember that though we drifted into empire in the east, we drifted out of it in the west, when a question of tariffs in 1776 lost us the American colonies, and a hundred years later those colonies were still suffering from the internecine strife that again rose out of a question of tariffs, though the slavery question was the stalking horse selected.

India can never be the home of the Anglo-Saxon yeoman. It is a magnificent field for the cultivation of the military and administrative talent among intellectually selected specimens of our upper classes. The birthright of the British yeoman, the broad lands of our colonies, were of necessity ceded with responsible government to the Colonial legislatures. The Crown lands no longer belong to the Crown of Great Britain, and this is the main impediment to any extensive system of organized military emigration. Yet as it is manifestly to the advantage of the colonies that there should be an organized system of emigration, instead of leaving them to the unhappy-go-unlucky want of system by which stowaways and criminals, effeminate clerks, and gentlemen whose heads are sometimes as soft as their hands, may drift to their shores.

Hitherto the military emigration of British officers and soldiers has failed because it was based on wrong principles, and that lately attempted by Canada herself in giving grants of land to the time-expired soldiers of the battalions sent for service to Fort Garry, has benefited nobody but land speculators, because it was based upon broad republican principles, which do not suit soldiers or men habituated to discipline. An indiscriminate grant or land order for 160 acres was given to officers and men alike. The grant had a name, but no local habitation; its whereabouts was not defined; to the mind of the supposed settler it might turn out a shaking swamp (muskeg), a strip of alkaline desert, or an uncleared wilderness of valueless wood. No officer of sense or self-respect would think of settling down on an equality with Tommy Atkins and Mrs. T., to whose husband he had so lately administered pack-drill. Unscrupulous officers were tempted to buy the prospective claims of these men for the price of a few bottles of old rye whisky, not because *bonâ fide* settlers, but to hold, and subsequently to sell, to land speculators. I am speaking with a knowledge of facts.

Again, the old colonization by Imperial troops was based on the idea that every soldier, after perhaps twenty-one years' hard service, mainly in tropical climates, was fit, in comparatively old age, to blossom into a successful colonial farmer, no matter what his antecedents—being without capital, energy, or agricultural experience. The first or second semi-arctic winter of Canada drove him to despair and drink, to which military service in old times only too frequently predisposed a man. As for the officers, not having been in the first instance granted estates commensurate with their rank, and having spent most of their capital or retired pay in the purchase of land, they sank to the level of the rank and file, and their sons, often without proper education, intermarried with the daughters of the ordinary working population, or in some cases of their fathers' servants, who eventually owned the farm on which they had been hired to work. Canada is strewn with the wrecks of the families of British officers. Of course there are exceptions to every rule. One of the most striking is that of the descendants of the 79th Highlanders, officers and men, disbanded after the war in 1760, settled at Murray Bay, near Quebec. Fifteen years afterwards they left their farms to march against the Americans invading Canada, and returned to their ploughshares when they sheathed their victorious claymores.

The settlement of the 79th Highlanders was upon the old French feudal system. The colonel and officers were given signorial grants of land and magisterial privileges, and their descendants are still to be found loyal to the Crown, and curiously enough the signorial estates have devolved upon another officer of the 79th, nearly a century after the original settlement, by right of his wife, the daughter of the last seigneur. These privileges have been abolished.

The original settlers were not supplied with Scotch wives, and the amiable little French Canadian girls with whom they intermarried, made them good Catholics and happy fathers of a numerous progeny, still retaining the typical frame and vigour of the Scot though speaking in the softer tongue of France.

Emigration to the old province of Quebec is no longer required. The French Canadians have increased so rapidly as to have already emigrated in considerable numbers to the United States. And the fertile province of Ontario also has got far beyond the need of military emigration, but it is required to open up what will be the great grain-producing valley of the Saskatchewan with its coal-fields—a fertile belt of alluvial prairie soil with an acreage about equal to that of Spain, France, and England put together. Here such pioneers would be wanted in the first instance to build the Pacific railroad, guard the depôts of supplies, &c., form settlements along the route, and give military security against Indians at a cost that could scarcely, by any possibility, exceed what Canada already pays for her mounted military police, 1000 dollars per man per annum. Far less would be the cost of the passage of military settlers and their families with a supply of three years' rations and agricultural implements, while the covered carts that conveyed them to their location on their prairie home would give shelter until quarters were constructed. British Columbia, especially along its southern frontier and in Vancouver's Island, requires such military settlements, for manifest reasons it is not necessary to discuss. The climate is more favourable than that of any known colony, resembling England without the east wind. The same physical causes that have contributed to England's greatness will, to a certain extent, create in Vancouver's Island in no very remote future a prosperous country. The equable temperature produced by the equatorial current, corresponding in the Pacific to the Atlantic Gulf Stream, brings down the isothermal lines far south of the corresponding latitudes on the eastern coast, creating a climate that gives a maximum of working days in the year as against climates of extremes. Vancouver's Island and British Columbia is as large as France and Ireland, but the arable area is contracted by the mountain ranges; but there are vast tracts of brush-grass suitable for herds that require no house wintering. The coal, iron, and gold, and splendid timber not far from a series of magnificent harbours, will make Vancouver a trade starting-point from America to Asia—as England has been from Europe to America. If there is any truth in Buckle's 'History of Civilization,' that Western Britain will be great! when the Californian, receiving no fresh blood from Europe, will have degenerated into the *sans-souciance* of southern Europeans.

This is the country that asks for secession for want of railway arterial connection with the heart of the Empire. It is too far for our population to reach it by the ordinary system of "drift."

www.ingramcontent.com/pod-product-compliance
Lightning Source LLC
Chambersburg PA
CBHW032000230426
43672CB00010B/2222